The Masala Cookbook

Parvati Narshi and Ben Williams

The Masala Cookbook

Parvati Narshi and Ben Williams

First published in 2005 by Struik Publishers
(a division of New Holland Publishing
(South Africa) (Pty) Ltd)
New Holland Publishing is a member of
Johnnic Communications Ltd
Cornelis Struik House, 80 McKenzie Street,
Cape Town 8001
86-88 Edgware Road, London,
W2 2EA, United Kingdom
14 Aquatic Drive, Frenchs Forest,
NSW 2086, Australia
218 Lake Road, Northcote, Auckland,
New Zealand

www.struik.co.za

Publishing manager: Linda de Villiers
Mananging editor: Cecilia Barfield
Editor: Irma van Wyk
Designer: Helen Henn
Photographer: Melody Deas
Food stylists: Brita du Plessis; Vo Pollard
Proofreader and indexer: Joy Clack

Reproduction by Hirt & Carter Cape
(Pty) Ltd
Printed and bound by Sing Cheong
Printing Company Limited, Hong Kong

ISBN 1 86872 977 X

10 9 8 7 6 5 4 3 2 1

The authors and publishers would like to thank the
following for the loan of their homeware products:
@home, Block & Chisel, Bright House,
Chinaworks@Block & Chisel, House and Interiors,
Lim, Loft Living, Loads of Living, L'Orangerie,
Moroccan Warehouse, Plush Bazaar

www.imagesofafrica.co.za
IMAGES OF AFRICA
PHOTO LIBRARY
Log on to our photographic website
www.imagesofafrica.co.za for an
African experience

Dedicated to C.N. 1935–1995

The authors wish to thank Jyoti, Hament, Jayshree, Chitra, Melissa
and Doug for their love, support and encouragement.

Contents

Introduction

Just as the French culinary tradition has its demi-glace and hollandaise 'mother sauces', so Indian cuisine has a set of elementary spice and chilli blends – the masalas – which comprise the source of boundless kitchen inspiration. Know the masala alphabet of just four letters, and you can jump right into an entire culinary language. With masalas to hand, you're just a scoop or a sprinkle away from becoming a true 'curry genius'!

The Masala Cookbook starts with the A-B-Cs. You meet the main masalas first, four mouth-watering mixtures that give your efforts the true Indian 'touch': Red Masala, Green Masala, Three-spice Masala and Warm Masala. These are the keys to the 1-2-3s that follow, the scrumptious curries, dhals, gourmet productions and savoury bites that invariably cause exclamations of pleasure when served.

After the main dishes, it's time for a treat. Chapter 5 – Tea Break – introduces two 'sweet' masalas, which make the perfect cup of soothing, restorative 'Chai' (p.121), and the heavenly indulgences that are Indian sweetmeats. You'll also find rice and bread recipes inside, so that every dish may be served complete.

Simplicity, healthfulness, vibrant tastes and colours: these are the themes of contemporary cooking, and are the precise results of the magical masala system introduced here. Quick, dazzling Indian food is now never out of reach. Enjoy!

Parvati Narshi and Ben Williams
June 2005

A NOTE ON MEASUREMENTS

Firstly, all teaspoons (tsp = 5 ml) and tablespoons (Tbsp = 15 ml) are level, unless indicated otherwise. Secondly, you'll see from many recipes in this book that onions, tomatoes and potatoes are major building blocks in Indian cuisine. All three vary widely in size and type – we've stuck to the following standards for our ingredient lists:

'The Standard Onion'

The standard onion is a golden charmer: it is bulbous, very firm, well-protected in thin, papery skin, and weighs between 150 and 170 grams, which is on the medium-to-small side. Avoid white onions and pickle onions. When recipes call for onions to be 'finely chopped', they mean it! The finer the better. Many recipes require onions to be braised 'until golden brown and cooked through', an effect which is achieved at differing rates and temperatures, depending on your stove and pots and pans. You'll want to note your own cooking time and stove settings when braising onions, so that you can eventually cook them to perfection blindfolded.

'The Standard Tomato'

The standard tomato is juicily ripe and deep red, firm but 'pressable', and smells wonderfully. fruity and 'tomato-y'. It weighs between 100 and 130 grams, which is on the small side. Avoid rock-hard tomatoes and those that are orange or yellow in colour. It's good to keep a few tomatoes ripening on a sunlit windowsill, so that you never lack for super-red colour in your curries.

'The Standard Potato'

The standard potato is a squeaky-clean trooper, a 'baking' potato with or without a brown jacket, weighing between 150 and 170 grams, which is medium size. Potatoes should be very firm. Avoid any with eyes or dark spots, and note that none of our recipes call for any but the 'baking' variety: no baby, new or sweet potatoes.

CONVERSION TABLE

Metric	US cups	Imperial
5 ml	1 tsp	$^{3}/_{16}$ fl oz
15 m	1 Tbsp	½ fl oz
60 ml	4 Tbsp/¼ cup	2 fl oz
80 ml	⅓ cup	2¾ fl oz
125 ml	½ cup	4½ fl oz
160 ml	⅔ cup	5½ fl oz
200 ml	¾ cup	7 fl oz
250 ml	1 cup	9 fl oz
100 g		3½ oz
250 g		9 oz
500 g		1 lb
750 g		1¾ lb
1 kg		2¼ lb

Pan Spices and Other Ingredients

It's impossible to be too choosy about your spices. In cooking, you reap what you sow – and you'll reap sumptuous rewards if you buy good, whole spices to grind at home. No batch of spices is completely perfect, but at the very least they should be bone-dry and have a fresh, pungent smell. Be on the lookout for the best batches: large, sleek seeds are preferable to small or shrivelled ones, and first prize is the discovery of a batch that is virginally clean – free of dirt, dust, sticks and chaff, all of which can mar flavour. Buy extra! A batch of clean spices is a splendid treasure.

The list that follows is a complete glossary of the essential ingredients featured in this book. Some are for masalas only, some are for 'pan spices' – braised in the pan in oil or ghee at the start of a recipe – and some are used for both.

TOP ROW (left to right): Cardamom, Chillies, Dried Chillies, Crushed Chillies and Chilli Powder, Cinnamon Sticks, Cloves, Coriander Seeds and Fresh Coriander, Cumin Seeds, Curry Leaves
BOTTOM ROW (left to right): Fennel, Ghee, Fresh and Dried Ginger, Mustard Seeds, Nutmeg, Paprika, White and Black Pepper, Star Anise, Turmeric

asafoetida (powder)

A dark-yellow spice that is prized as an important digestive aid. It is often used in vegetarian dishes as a 'pan spice'. The slightly offensive pungency changes to a more subtle flavour during cooking.

cardamom pods

Powerful and versatile, cardamom is used in the Warm and Tea Masalas, many meat and poultry dishes, and sweetmeats. It is generally sold as a green pod – the plumper and less wrinkled the better – and ground or cooked whole. For sweet dish recipes (including 'Cardamom-Nutmeg Masala', p. 120), however, only the small black seeds inside the pods are used.

CAUTION WHEN ROASTING: Cardamom seeds blister easily when overheated, and should never be roasted outside of their pods in the microwave, or beyond the 5-minute threshold. When roasting, always inspect the batch when you pause to stir it, checking to see if any pods have blackened or blistered. If so, stop roasting, and open a few 'good' pods to make sure the entire batch hasn't been affected. Never roast cardamom pods on any setting above 200W/low/defrost.

chilli (fresh and dried)

The well-known pod of the *Capsicum* genus of plants. Chillies come in all shapes, sizes and colours. In this book, we use cayenne chillies, which are the base ingredients in the Red and Green Masalas. See the introduction to these masalas for more detail (p. 15).

chilli (powder)

Dried red chillies ground to an industrial-grade fineness. Test different chilli powders to find one you like. Excellent for extra colour and tang.

chillies (crushed)

Terrifically hot, dried, crushed red cayenne chillies, essential for making Red Masala in small batches.

cinnamon sticks

The inner bark of the cinnamon tree, used in many curries. Thin bark is preferable, both for its flavour and ease of snapping into small bits (which is best for both cooking and grinding).

cloves

Perhaps the most powerful spice of all. Used often but in very small quantities, mostly whole as a 'pan spice' (especially in meat dishes), and also finely ground in Warm Masala.

coriander seeds

A smooth, rich and highly aromatic spice, of the utmost importance in Indian cuisine. Like cumin, it is foundational in both the Three-Spice and Warm Masalas.

coriander (fresh)

Also known as 'dhania', 'cilantro' and 'Chinese parsley'. An essential herb in Indian cuisine, especially finely chopped as a garnish for curries. Wash thoroughly to remove any sand. Remove and discard root ends; chop stalks up finely with the leaves.

cumin seeds

A strong, savoury spice, one of the most important in Indian cuisine. Like coriander, foundational in both Three-spice and Warm Masalas. Seeds often feature as 'pan spices'.

curry leaves (fresh or dried)

Used in many curries and indispensable in seafood dishes. The fresh leaves are preferable to the dried. Store fresh leaves, wrapped in tissue or kitchen paper, in a plastic container in the fridge.

fennel seeds

A specialised sweet spice, required almost exclusively as an ingredient in Warm Masala. It tastes like liquorice.

fenugreek seeds

Small, squarish, dark-yellow seeds used almost solely as a 'pan spice' and essential in seafood dishes. Very sensitive to heat: when braising, ensure they don't sizzle too long in oil or ghee, or they'll blacken and scorch.

fenugreek (fresh)

A leafy herb that resembles fresh coriander, fenugreek is more savoury in flavour and usually a darker shade of green. Only the leaves should be used, not the stalks.

ganthoda

Also known as 'pipramul', 'piper longum' and 'long pepper'. A woody twig that is sweet like fennel and strong like pepper. Used exclusively in this book as an ingredient in Tea Masala.

ghee

Clarified butter. Ghee and oil are interchangeable in most recipes, although ghee's rich, nutty flavour is preferable.

ginger (dried)

A 'petrified' version of the fresh root, usually white in colour.

ginger (powder)

Dried ginger ground to an industrial-grade fineness. Used exclusively in Tea Masala in this book.

mustard seeds

An essential 'pan spice'. The seeds 'pop' in hot oil, and are lively in flavour. Keep them in large quantities. Once they start 'popping', it's definitely time to move on to the next step!

nutmeg

Best bought as a whole 'nut', then grated as required using the 'star' face of a grater, or pounded in a mortar until fine. Very hard and very moist, it should never be ground in a spice or coffee grinder – it can damage the machine and scorch the spice. The exception to this rule is the Warm Masala recipe, which requires the nutmeg to be well roasted and pulverised before grinding.

paprika

A condiment made from dried red sweet peppers. Similar in colour to chilli powder, but usually much less strong (hot). Used primarily for its colour.

pepper (black)

A 'dirty' spice that requires much sorting (for sticks, empty husks, etc.) and tossing (in a wire strainer, to dislodge the chaff) before grinding. A clean batch of large, hard, black peppercorns is invaluable!

pepper (white)

Subtly and deliciously different from black pepper, whitish-grey in colour, and used chiefly in Tea Masala.

saffron

The stigma of the crocus flower, a tiny reddish-orange filament often worth more than its weight in gold. It imparts a uniquely rich and satisfying flavour and colour, intensified by soaking the saffron in a little hot water for several minutes. Saffron may be stored in the deep freeze.

CLOCKWISE (from top left): Asafoetida, Tynol (Ajowan), Ganthoda, Fenugreek Seeds and Fresh Fenugreek
ABOVE SPOON: Saffron

star anise

The many-pointed star anise pod is ground along with its seeds. A deliciously enticing spice, key to Warm Masala's dark, sweet flavour.

turmeric (powder)

Bright, dark orange, essential for imparting warmth of colour to most dishes. It is used in small quantities because of its deep dyeing properties. Wash your fingers after touching it.

tynol seeds

Also known as 'ajowan', 'ajmo', 'carom' and 'Bishop's weed'. This is a tiny brown seed that imparts a zesty flavour and is used as a 'pan spice' in certain vegetarian curries.

The Four Masalas

Red and Green Masalas are potent,
chilli-based pastes that add instant tang and
colour to curry creations. Tiny amounts of
Three-spice and Warm Masalas bring incredible
richness of flavour to food.

quick chutneys relishes yoghurt dishes

The secret to preparing Indian dishes that delight the palate – without requiring elaborate fuss – lies in the four masalas presented here: Red Masala, Green Masala, Three-spice Masala and Warm Masala.

The term 'masala' is often thought to refer to powders only. Not so: Red and Green Masalas are moist pastes – and quite possibly the most ingenious curry ingredients ever invented! Three-Spice and Warm Masalas are more familiar, being dry mixtures of roasted coriander, cumin and other seeds, but they are far superior to anything found in a store. A little masala, it seems, goes on forever – use them in small scoops and sprinkles, and savour the princely results.

The 'science' of making good masala is not exact, but it is governed by a few rules. Spices must be clean: free of husks, chaff and sticks. Never use pre-ground spices in these masalas. Fresh ingredients like garlic and ginger should be super-fresh: firm and smooth to the touch with crisp but tender flesh. It's good to test your masalas soon after you've made them: each batch is slightly different. The first dish, followed according to the recipe, will tell you if the batch to hand is strong (too hot!), or weak (too bland!), and you can adjust amounts accordingly. This chapter finishes with easy recipes for delicious chutneys, relishes and yoghurt dishes, the perfect starting place to test your new masalas.

Red and Green Masalas

Prized for their bright colours and vivid aromas, Red and Green Masalas are possibly the best-kept secrets in all of Indian cuisine. Half the ingredients and flavours needed to prepare a curry *par excellence* can be found in a teaspoon or less of one or the other. And they keep in the deep freeze for up to a year – keeping superb Indian cooking within your reach at all times.

Red Masala is the 'master masala'. Nearly every savoury dish in this book calls for it. Best prepared in ample quantities, it will become one of your most trusted kitchen aids. Green Masala is Red Masala's more delicate cousin, used particularly when a dish calls for a vibrant green colour, or when the 'bite' of green chillies is needed in preference to the 'tang' of red ones. The two masalas are also sometimes used in combination.

The secret to both is the quality of the chillies used to make them. Cayennes, like other chillies, change from green to red as they mature on their stalks. Green Masala is made from the less mature, less hot, green chillies, and Red Masala from the green and more mature red chillies, plus red chillies that have been dried.

When buying fresh chillies, select pods that are as bright in colour as possible. To test for freshness, break the skin of a pod lightly with your thumbnail, press your finger to the broken skin, and then lightly to your tongue. The taste of the chilli should pack a piercing punch! Your thumbnail will also tell you how crisp the chilli's skin is. Green cayenne pods should be especially firm, packed to bursting with seeds.

Dried chillies, meanwhile, are extremely potent – avoid touching them and even their packaging with your bare hands. They should be whole (as opposed to broken husks mixed with loose seeds) and deep red, with as little discoloration as possible. Bag them in double or triple layers before taking them home, and make your masala soon after buying them.

Hints and variations

Never rub your eyes, stroke a pet, or wipe a child's nose after handling chillies, fresh or dry!

The availability of cayenne chillies can vary with the seasons. If you can't find them, you'll probably see other varieties for sale. You can make the Red and Green Masalas with any strong chilli of medium-to-small size.

One of the joys of these masalas is their distinctive aroma, an evergreen intensity which rushes to your nose with the same freshness each time you open the lid. If, after several months, the aroma begins to fade, it's time for a new batch.

Red Masala

Preparation time: 35 minutes (large batch) 15 minutes (small batch)

LARGE BATCH
30 g garlic
60 g ginger root
water for soaking
50 g dried red chillies
25 g fresh red chillies
40 g fresh green chillies
1½ tsp lemon juice
2 Tbsp salt
1 Tbsp oil

1. Soak the garlic and ginger in water for 10 minutes for ease of peeling. De-stalk the dried red chillies (don't overhandle them – wear kitchen gloves), and place in a medium-sized bowl filled with lukewarm water, immersing about three quarters of the chillies; stir to wet them all. Collect any spilled seeds and add them to the soaking chillies. Soak for 15 minutes until soft. De-stalk the fresh red and green chillies, and soak in a separate bowl for 10 minutes.

2. Drain the garlic and ginger. Peel the garlic and scrape the ginger clean of skin with a serrated knife or the edge of a spoon, until shiny and yellow. Rinse, then dice, removing any dark spots or stems.

3. Drain the dried chillies in a colander placed in a bowl to collect spilled seeds. Return the seeds to the chillies. Drain the fresh chillies, and slice into quarters, careful not to touch the sliced chilli flesh. (Be sure to wash your hands after this step.) Mince all the chillies in a food processor to a coarse paste, first on low speed, then on high.

Add the ginger, then the garlic, mincing until the paste is even and mainly smooth. Stir the paste every now and again to ensure evenness.

4. Scoop the paste into a mixing bowl. Pour the lemon juice into the food processor to 'clean' out the last of the paste, then add this to the bowl and stir well. Mix in the salt until dissolved, and then the oil.

Red Masala should be an even, glistening, slightly dark red paste with a strong chilli aroma. Store it in an airtight container in the deep freeze, where it will keep for up to one year. Note that because of the masala's salt and oil, it never freezes completely solid, and may be scooped straight from its container.

SMALL BATCH

1 tsp finely chopped fresh red chillies
1 Tbsp finely chopped fresh green chillies
½ tsp finely chopped garlic
1 tsp finely chopped ginger root
2 tsp crushed chillies
½ tsp salt
¼ tsp paprika

1. Soak, sort, clean and peel all ingredients as indicated in the large-batch recipe. (Note that the small batch does not call for whole dried chillies.) Chop the chillies, garlic and ginger until very fine. (You may wish to wear kitchen gloves.)

2. Mix the fresh chillies, crushed chillies, garlic, ginger and salt in a mortar. Pound to a fine, even paste. Scoop the paste into a small bowl, add the paprika and stir in.

A small batch yields enough Red Masala to prepare two to three recipes.

Hints and variations

If you're making both Red and Green Masala at the same time (this is recommended – you save effort), start with the Green Masala. If you prepare the Red Masala first, the flavour and heat of its dried chillies will spike the Green Masala. Remember to test your masalas soon after they have been made with a simple recipe (for instance, 'Savoury Spinach', p. 57), so you can gauge their strength.

Green Masala

Preparation time: 25 minutes (large batch) 15 minutes (small batch)

LARGE BATCH
25 g garlic
50 g ginger root
water for soaking
125 g fresh green chillies
½ Tbsp lemon juice
1 Tbsp salt
1 tsp oil

1. Soak the garlic and ginger in water for 10 minutes for ease of peeling. Meanwhile, de-stalk the fresh green chillies, rinse and drain. Peel the garlic and scrape the ginger clean of skin with a serrated knife or the edge of a spoon, until shiny and yellow. Rinse both, then dice, removing any dark spots or stems.

2. Slice the chillies into quarters, careful not to touch the sliced chilli flesh. (Wash your hands after this step.) Mince the chillies in a food processor to a coarse paste, first on low speed, then on high. Add the ginger in batches, then the garlic, mincing until the paste is mostly smooth. Stir the paste every now and again to ensure evenness.

3. Scoop the paste into a mixing bowl. Add the lemon juice and salt, and stir until the salt has dissolved. Add the oil and mix in thoroughly.

Green Masala should be an even, glistening, bright green paste with a fresh, pungent chilli aroma. Store in an airtight container in the deep freeze, where it will keep for up to one year. Note that because of the masala's salt and oil, it never freezes completely solid, and may be scooped straight from its container.

SMALL BATCH

3 Tbsp (24–30 g or 6–10 medium chillies)
finely chopped fresh green chillies
2½ tsp finely chopped ginger root
½ tsp finely chopped garlic
1 tsp salt

1. Soak, sort, clean and peel the ingredients as indicated in the large-batch recipe. Chop the chillies, garlic and ginger until very fine. (Be sure to wash your hands after this step.)

2. Mix all the ingredients in a mortar and pound to a fine, even paste.

A small batch yields enough Green Masala to prepare two to three recipes.

Hints and variations

A batch of overly dark green chillies may be lightened with 10–20 g of fresh red ones. Remember to test your masalas soon after they have been made with a simple recipe (for instance, 'Raita', p. 29), so that you can gauge their strength.

Three-spice and Warm Masalas

These two dry masalas outwardly resemble the kind available in small packets in shops and huge heaps at markets, but they are incomparably superior to other powders: more fragrant, more flavoursome, and much more effective. Use them and your cooking will reach new levels of exquisiteness!

Three-spice is just that: Indian cuisine's two most prominent seeds, coriander and cumin, and a third, which adds 'body' to the mixture's 'nose', black pepper kernels. Just a sprinkle of this masala delivers buttery richness and a subtle, piquant flavour to the largest pot of food. Three-spice is all-purpose – it pays to make it in all-purpose-sized batches.

Warm Masala is more complex, made of combinations of strong, mild and sweet spices, and often plays the role of 'finishing touch'. The 'Warm' in Warm Masala derives from the mixture's unique kind of strength: it's not 'hot' in the least.

(We believe that the warm feeling of satisfaction it gives every mouthful must be a factor, too!)

The key to both masalas lies in the roasting of their individual spices. Fortunately, this is a cinch! It takes just a few minutes in the microwave, and meanwhile your kitchen is flooded with the spices' indescribably delicious aromas. Roasted spices not only taste better, they also grind better, because they are drier.

When preparing individual spices for roasting, work in a well-lit area. Remove as much chaff, husks and 'dirt' as possible to ensure that maximum, undiluted flavour carries through to the masalas. Sort the spices on a white, microwave-safe plate and toss them thoroughly in a wire strainer. After roasting, remember not to grind the spices ultra finely: a hint of coarseness is the mark of a superior masala.

Three-spice Masala

Preparation time: 30 minutes (large batch) 5 minutes (small batch)

LARGE BATCH

50 g or about 11 Tbsp coriander seeds
20 g or about 3 Tbsp cumin seeds
10 g or about 1½ Tbsp black pepper kernels

1. Clean and sort the coriander, cumin and black pepper separately, removing any sticks, stones or husks. Toss the spices separately in a wire strainer to sift out any chaff.

2. Pour the spices on to a large microwave-safe tray or dish, mix and spread out into a thin, even layer. Roast on 200W/low/defrost for 5–6 minutes, until the mixture is warm and produces a pleasant aroma. Pause roasting twice to stir thoroughly. Cool in the microwave for 3 minutes.

3. While the spice mixture is still warm, grind it to a semi-fine powder in three batches, pausing several times to stir each batch.

Three-spice Masala should be golden brown and slightly coarse, leaving a fine powdery residue when touched. Store it in a cool, dry place. Its mellow flavour will keep for up to one year.

SMALL BATCH

2½ tsp coriander seeds
¼ tsp cumin seeds
⅛ tsp black pepper kernels

1. Clean and sort the spices as indicated in the large-batch recipe instructions.

2. Roast the spices together in the microwave on 200W/low/defrost for 4–5 minutes. Pound well in a mortar.

A small batch yields enough Three-spice Masala to prepare three to four dishes.

Warm Masala

Preparation time: 40 minutes (large batch) 20 minutes (small batch)

Warm Masala is also known as garam masala.

LARGE BATCH

15 g or about 2 Tbsp cumin seeds
50 g or about 11 Tbsp coriander seeds
20 g or about 3½ Tbsp fennel seeds
15 g or about 2 Tbsp black pepper kernels
15 g cinnamon stick pieces or about 3 Tbsp small pieces
½ tsp whole cloves
½ medium nutmeg
2–3 star anise pods (whole)
10 g or about 1½ Tbsp cardamom pods

1. Prepare the masala's mild spices. Clean and sort the cumin, coriander and fennel seeds and toss them separately in a wire strainer. Pour these spices on to a microwave-safe plate or tray and spread out into a thin, even layer. Roast on 200W/low/defrost for 5–6 minutes, pausing three times to stir. Set aside.

2. Prepare the strong spices. Clean and sort the black pepper, tossing the kernels in a wire strainer several times to sift out chaff and dirt. Break the cinnamon sticks into small pieces. Mix the cinnamon, black pepper and cloves on a micro-wave-safe plate or tray, and roast in one batch, as per step 1.

3. Prepare the sweet spices. Crush the nutmeg into small pieces in a mortar. Roast with the star anise and cardamom pods in one batch as per step 1. (See roasting caution for cardamom, p. 9.)

4. Grind the roasted mild spices in two batches, pausing several times to stir, until mostly fine. Reserve in a small mixing bowl. Pound the roasted strong spices in the mortar until coarsely crushed, then grind in one batch until fine. (The cloves will be coarser than the rest.) Reserve. Pound the roasted sweet spices in the mortar until coarsely crushed and then grind until mostly fine.

5. Mix all the spices together, stirring thoroughly.

Warm Masala should be a reddish-brown, somewhat coarse powder with an aroma that is both savoury and sweet. Store in a spice jar in a cool, dry place. It will retain its strength for up to one year.

SMALL BATCH

¼ tsp cumin seeds

2 tsp coriander seeds

½ tsp fennel seeds

⅛ tsp black pepper kernels

4–5 cinnamon stick pieces

3 whole cloves

4–5 cardamom pods

pinch grated nutmeg

1. Clean and sort all the spices as indicated in the large-batch recipe instructions. Cut the cloves into small pieces with a sharp knife.

2. Roast the cumin, coriander and fennel seeds in the microwave on 200W/low/defrost for 4–5 minutes. Pause to stir twice. Pound to fine in a mortar and set aside.

3. Roast the black pepper, cinnamon stick pieces and cloves in the microwave on 200W/low/defrost for 4–5 minutes. Pound to fine in the mortar and set aside.

4. Roast the cardamom pods in the microwave on 200W/low/defrost for 3–4 minutes. (See roasting caution for cardamom, p. 9.) Pound to fine in the mortar (remove husks which don't pulverise, if desired). Add the nutmeg to the mortar with the cardamom. Mix thoroughly.

5. Add the other pounded spices to the mortar with the cardamom and nutmeg, and mix thoroughly. Pound for a further 30 seconds to 1 minute to ensure optimal blending.

A small batch yields enough Warm Masala for about four to five dishes.

Hints and variations

It's important to wipe the mortar clean with a dry cloth between steps. Thin, flimsy cinnamon sticks are preferable to thick ones – they're easier to roast and grind, and more potent.

Quick Coriander Chutney

Preparation time: 10 minutes Yields ± 1 cup
Green Masala

This is a strong, salty, dry-ish chutney, which is an excellent table condiment for all occasions, and is particularly delicious with meat and poultry dishes. Try to use coriander with long, fresh stalks when you prepare it: the stalks contain good flavour and make the chutney easier to blend.

¾ cup skinless peanuts
50 g or about 1 cup coarsely chopped fresh coriander
6 coarsely chopped cloves garlic
½ tsp cumin seeds
1½ tsp Green Masala
2 Tbsp lemon juice
¼ tsp chilli powder
1 tsp salt

1. Pour the peanuts on to a microwave-safe dish or tray and spread them out evenly. Roast on 200W/low/defrost for 4–5 minutes, until they radiate heat and aroma. Pound the peanuts in a mortar until well crushed.

2. Place the coriander, garlic, cumin seeds and Green Masala in a food processor or liquidiser and add the lemon juice. Blend well on medium speed and pour into a bowl.

3. Add the peanuts and chilli powder and stir in thoroughly. Adjust to taste for salt and 'tang' (heat – extra Green Masala or chilli powder).

Serve on any occasion, especially with meat and poultry.

Hints and variations

For a more exotic chutney, add 1 Tbsp shredded coconut with the other ingredients at the beginning of step 1. To sweeten the chutney, add a few sprigs of mint. If it does not blend well, add extra lemon juice.

Thick Tomato Chutney

Preparation time: 5 minutes Yields ± 2 cups
Green Masala

For best results when preparing this sweet, sharp chutney, choose very red, very ripe tomatoes, and coriander with long stalks. Never liquidise the chopped onion with the other ingredients, because the chutney will become too watery. This chutney goes especially well with 'Mince Kebabs' (p. 81) and 'Foulka' (p. 156).

4 coarsely chopped tomatoes

4 coarsely chopped cloves garlic

40 g or about ¾ cup finely chopped fresh coriander

1½ tsp Green Masala

1½ tsp cumin seeds

1 Tbsp lemon juice

1½ tsp salt

2 tsp sugar

1 Tbsp brown vinegar

1½ tsp chilli powder

¼ coarsely chopped onion

1. Place the tomatoes, garlic, coriander, Green Masala and cumin seeds in a liquidiser. Add the lemon juice. Blend on low speed until the ingredients are well mixed but not entirely liquidised. Pour the ingredients into a mixing bowl. Stir in the salt, sugar, vinegar and chilli powder. Adjust to taste for salt, sweetness and 'tang' (strength – extra Green Masala or chilli powder). Reserve in the fridge.

2. Before serving, stir in the chopped onion.

Hints and variations

To give this chutney extra 'bite,' add ½ tsp finely chopped green chilli with the other ingredients at the beginning of step 1. For a fresh, sweet taste, add a few sprigs of mint to the liquidiser.

Green Masala Buttermilk

Preparation time: 10 minutes Serves 4–6
Green Masala

This super-simple side dish – only two steps – is a must for the table when biryani is on the menu (see 'Prawn Biryani', p. 106).

¼ tsp cumin seeds
¾ cup plain yoghurt
¼ cup water
¼ tsp Green Masala
¼ tsp salt
6–7 torn or lightly crushed curry leaves
(fresh or dried)
1 heaped Tbsp finely chopped fresh coriander

TO GARNISH
chilli powder or paprika

1. Pound the cumin seeds in a mortar until fine.

2. Combine all the ingredients in a liquidiser and blend on high until smooth. Reserve in the fridge.

Serve in a pitcher or individual bowls. Garnish with chilli powder or paprika before serving.

Raita

Preparation time: 15 minutes Serves 4
Green Masala

Raita is well-known for its fire-quenching properties: the yoghurt and cucumber soothe mouths burning from hot chillies! You don't strictly need to use the muslin cloth called for in step 2 – you'll simply have a somewhat thinner result. This dish best accompanies curries that are served with rice, but is suitable for all occasions.

350 g English cucumber (about ¾ medium cucumber, or 1½ cups unsqueezed cucumber gratings)
2 tsp mustard seeds
1½ tsp cumin seeds
10 Tbsp or about ⅔ cup plain yoghurt
½ tsp salt
1 tsp Green Masala
pinch turmeric
1½ tsp mustard powder (optional)
5–6 torn or lightly crushed curry leaves (fresh or dried)
1 heaped Tbsp finely chopped fresh coriander

1. Peel the cucumber lengthwise, leaving thin strips of skin for a 'zebra' effect. (The skin enhances the colour of the dish.)

2. Line a bowl with a muslin cloth of double thickness. Grate the cucumber into the muslin, gather the cloth together and squeeze out most of the juice. Put the gratings in a bowl.

3. Pound the mustard seeds in a mortar until very fine. Remove and set aside. Pound the cumin seeds in the mortar, leaving slightly coarse. Mix with the mustard seeds.

4. Add the yoghurt to the grated cucumber and mix thoroughly. Add the salt, Green Masala, turmeric, mustard powder, crushed mustard and cumin seeds, and mix well. Add the curry leaves and coriander and mix in thoroughly.

Reserve in the fridge for 30 minutes, allowing the yoghurt to absorb the flavour of the spices. Serve as an accompaniment to most curries, dhals, rice, and so on.

Hints and variations

Raita is best prepared with the creamiest part of the yoghurt (on the lid and edges of the container). In place of mustard seeds, simply add 2 tsp mustard spread. Thicken Raita with extra yoghurt. Alternative: use carrot gratings instead of cucumber, or the two combined.

Soft-boiled Egg and Tomato Relish

Preparation time: 10 minutes Cooking time: 15 minutes Serves 4
Red Masala, Three-spice Masala, Warm Masala

This dish is often served as a spicy relish to go with a variety of meat curries and vegetable dhals, but it makes for a great stand-alone curry, too. If you have leftovers, use it as a sandwich spread: it's delicious between two slices of brown bread!

5 large eggs
1½ Tbsp oil
½ finely chopped onion
1 finely diced potato
¼ cup water
½ tsp salt
¼ tsp Red Masala
¼ tsp turmeric
½ tsp Three-spice Masala
1½ grated tomatoes
½ Tbsp finely chopped fresh coriander
1 finely sliced tomato

PAN SPICE
¼ tsp fenugreek seeds

TO GARNISH
¼ tsp Warm Masala
1 heaped Tbsp finely chopped fresh coriander

1. Soft-boil the eggs: bring 2–3 cups of water to the boil, then reduce to a simmer. Lower the eggs one-by-one into the water with a spoon, return the water to a gentle boil and cover partially. Boil for 6–7 minutes, remove the eggs and reserve until cool enough to handle. Carefully peel off the shell and thick white outer skin.

2. Heat the oil on medium-high. When hot, add the fenugreek seeds, stir once and allow to sizzle for 20 seconds. Add the onion, stir well and cover. Braise for 3–5 minutes until golden brown and thoroughly cooked. Stir occasionally.

3. Reduce the heat. Add the diced potato, water, salt, Red Masala and turmeric, and stir well. Add the Three-spice Masala, cover and simmer for 10 minutes.

4. Add the grated tomatoes and fresh coriander and stir, then add the sliced tomato. Cover and simmer for 5 minutes.

5. Slice the eggs in half lengthwise with a sharp knife and lower them into the relish with a spoon, yolk-side up. Spoon the relish lightly over the eggs, cover and continue to simmer for 2–3 minutes.

Garnish with Warm Masala and coriander. Serve warm as a side dish, especially to accompany dhal dishes.

Hints and variations
Note: this dish does not reheat well in the microwave – the eggs become rubbery.

Khari

Cooking time: 20 minutes Serves 4
Green Masala

A warm, savoury yoghurt dish, Khari is tried-and-true comfort food that will warm the heart as much as the stomach! Nothing transmits the aroma and flavour of Green Masala quite like it. Khari is a splendid accompaniment to any dish served with rice.

10 Tbsp or about ⅔ cup plain yoghurt
⅔ cup water
½ tsp salt
¾ tsp Green Masala
⅛ tsp turmeric
5–6 torn or lightly crushed curry leaves
(fresh or dried)
½ tsp sugar
3 Tbsp chickpea dhal flour (gram flour)
2 Tbsp oil

PAN SPICES
¼ tsp mustard seeds
¼ tsp cumin seeds
⅛ tsp fenugreek seeds

1. Spoon the yoghurt into a medium saucepan. Add the water and stir. Add the salt, Green Masala, turmeric, curry leaves and sugar. Stir well. (This mixture may be stored in the fridge for later cooking.)

2. Add the chickpea dhal flour to the yoghurt mixture and beat with a whisk until smooth.

3. Prepare the pan spices. Heat the oil in a second, small saucepan. When hot, add the pan spices, stir once and allow to sizzle for about 20 seconds. Pour the pan spices into the yoghurt mixture (it will hiss and splutter).

4. Immediately place the yoghurt saucepan on the hot stove plate, stir the mixture continuously for 30 seconds, then again every minute until it begins to boil. (Watch it closely – it may boil over.) When it starts to boil, remove the khari from the heat and cover to keep warm.

Serve warm with any rice dish.

Hints and variations
Cake (plain) flour may be used as a substitute for chickpea dhal flour if necessary.

Carrot Atchar

Preparation time: 5 minutes Cooking time: 10 minutes Yields ± 1½ cups

The saying goes that no Indian home is complete without atchar. This is one of the simplest and tastiest, and may be served with any dish. The recipe does not call for masala – a rarity in this book!

250–300 g carrots (about 3 large), peeled
and sliced into short thin sticks
1½ tsp salt
1½ tsp chilli powder
1½ Tbsp oil
1 Tbsp cornflour
2½ Tbsp water
4 Tbsp vinegar
2 Tbsp sugar

PAN SPICES
½ tsp mustard seeds
7–10 torn or lightly crushed curry leaves
(fresh or dried)

1. Place the carrot sticks in a wide mixing bowl. Add the salt and chilli powder and stir well.

2. Heat the oil in a small saucepan on medium. Add the mustard seeds. When sizzling, add the curry leaves and stir well. Add the cornflour and water, and stir continuously for 2–3 minutes until a gelatinous paste forms. Remove the saucepan from the heat.

3. Spoon the paste over the carrots. Add the vinegar and stir until the paste dissolves completely. Add the sugar and stir until dissolved. Adjust to taste for strength (chilli powder) and salt, and for sauce consistency by adding extra vinegar if desired.

The best result is an atchar that is not watery but nonetheless 'drips'. Serve as an accompaniment to most curries, especially those without much gravy. Store in the fridge. It will keep for several weeks.

Hints and variations
For a more pungent taste, roast ½ tsp fenugreek seeds for 4–5 minutes in the microwave on 200W/low/defrost. Pound in a mortar until fine, and add with the sugar in step 3.

Kumquat Atchar

Preparation time: 10 minutes Cooking time: 40 minutes Yields ± 2 cups

When kumquats are in season, this is a 'must-make' recipe. It's like an Indian version of marmalade, oozing sweetness and spice, and its bright colour enlivens any plate. Like 'Carrot Atchar' (p. 33), this is one of the few recipes in the book that does not require masala.

300 g kumquats (about 30)
⅓ cup white vinegar
¾ cup sugar
1 clove garlic, sliced into slivers
¼ tsp salt
¾ tsp crushed chillies or chilli powder
½ Tbsp oil

PAN SPICES
½ tsp mustard seeds
4–5 torn or lightly crushed curry leaves
(fresh or dried)
1 tsp sesame seeds

1. Rinse the kumquats thoroughly and drain well. Slice each kumquat in half lengthwise and remove all the pips.

2. Place the kumquats in a medium-sized saucepan and add the vinegar. Heat on high, stirring constantly until the vinegar begins to simmer. Reduce the heat. Simmer uncovered for 3–5 minutes until the kumquat rind is semi-soft.

3. Add the sugar and stir until dissolved. Continue to simmer for 10–12 minutes, until the liquid is syrupy. Pour the contents of the saucepan into a bowl, add the garlic slivers and stir well. Leave the kumquats to cool for 10 minutes. Add the salt and crushed chillies or chilli powder, stirring well.

4. Heat the oil in a small saucepan. When hot, add the mustard seeds, stir and allow to sizzle for about 15 seconds. Add the curry leaves and sesame seeds and stir well. Remove from the heat, pour over the kumquats and stir in.

Reserve the atchar overnight, if possible, to allow the kumquats to absorb the flavours of the spices. Serve as an accompaniment to any curry. Store in an airtight container in the fridge, where it will keep for several weeks.

Vegetarian Dishes

Dazzling variations on classic Indian dishes come to life when masalas are introduced to the humble root, legume and vegetable.

Vegetarian cooking is Indian cooking at its most versatile. The important place it has held in Indian culture down the centuries has led to a panoply of creative methods with the offerings of the vegetable market.

There are seemingly dozens of genres in vegetarian cooking: the recipes in this chapter are categorised into dhals, curries, bites and gourmet dishes. The results are positively gorgeous – and you can use your favourites as tasty references for further explorations. Dhals (pp. 39–44) are the lentils, or 'peas', of certain legumes, revered for their health and energy giving properties. They come in many different colours and sizes, and can't be beaten for simplicity of preparation or joy of eating. We feature three of the most popular dhals: moong (also called mung beans), chickpea dhal (also known as gram dhal, not to be confused with whole chickpeas), and 'oil' dhal (also known as toovar dhal or pigeon pea).

Next come the classic vegetable curries (pp. 45–59), many of which are considered 'dry' curries. This is a touch misleading: 'dry' simply means 'no gravy'. The dishes are sumptuously seasoned, delicately cooked versions of the raw originals. There are some scrumptious gravy curries in this section too.

The three quick veggie bites that follow (pp. 60–63) are terrific tantalisers – you'll be popping them into your mouth as you flip them out of the pan! And lastly, vegetarian cooking is taken up a notch with four 'gourmet' recipes at the end of the chapter (pp. 64–73). Each is a rewarding challenge, entailing extra steps, more attention to detail, and good planning. The inventiveness of Indian cuisine is on full display here: you are invited to join a world of delightful craftsmanship with delicious payoffs!

Chickpea Dhal with Spinach

Preparation time: 10 minutes Soaking time: 1 hour Cooking time: 45 minutes Serves 4
Red Masala, Warm Masala

Here chickpea dhal, also known as gram dhal, is simmered with spinach for a filling, flavoursome meal that you'll be happy to eat for supper, lunch the next day, and supper again!

1 cup chickpea (gram) dhal
3 cups water
¼ finely chopped onion
100 g or about 1 cup peeled and diced courgette
½ finely chopped tomato
40 g (about 2 large leaves) de-stalked and shredded spinach
½ Tbsp lemon juice
¾ tsp salt
¼ tsp turmeric
1½ Tbsp oil

PAN SPICES
2–3 cinnamon stick pieces
½ tsp mustard seeds
pinch asafoetida
½ tsp Red Masala

TO GARNISH
½ tsp Warm Masala
2 heaped Tbsp finely chopped fresh coriander

1. Rinse and drain the dhal. Cover with lukewarm water, soak for 1 hour and drain well.

2. Pour the drained dhal into a pot, add 2½ cups of water and bring to the boil. Reduce the heat and simmer, partially covered, for about 20 minutes, until the dhal is semi-tender.

3. Add the onion and courgette, then stir in the tomato, spinach, lemon juice, salt, turmeric and ½ cup water. Cover and simmer for 20 minutes, until thoroughly cooked.

4. Heat the oil in a small saucepan. When hot, add the cinnamon, mustard seeds, asafoetida and Red Masala. Stir once and allow to sizzle for about 10 seconds, then add to the dhal, which will splutter when it is poured in. 'Clean' the saucepan with 1 Tbsp water and a little dhal, and add this to the pot. Stir well, cover and simmer for 5 minutes. The dhal should now be thick and soupy.

Garnish with Warm Masala and coriander, and serve hot with 'Classic Roti' (p. 147).

Hints and variations
In a pinch, no soaking is necessary: merely extend the simmering in step 2 by about 30 minutes (adding extra water).

Whole Moong (Mung Beans)

Preparation time: 10 minutes Cooking time: 40 minutes Serves 4
Red Masala

Dhals are hulled lentils, so strictly speaking whole moong isn't one, because it keeps its shell. But as a delicious, superbly warming and filling dish, it deserves to be listed with the true dhals.

1 cup whole moong (mung beans)
3½ cups water
20 g or about ¼ cup finely diced butternut
½ finely chopped tomato
1½ tsp salt
¼ tsp Red Masala
½ tsp turmeric
1 tsp lemon juice
1 Tbsp oil

PAN SPICES
¼ tsp cumin seeds
⅛ tsp asafoetida
8–10 torn or lightly crushed curry leaves
(fresh or dried)
1 red chilli shell, de-seeded (optional)

TO GARNISH
2 heaped Tbsp finely chopped fresh coriander

1. Rinse the moong under a tap and drain. Pour it into a medium-sized pot and add the water. Cover and bring to the boil. Reduce the heat and simmer for about 20 minutes, until the moong begins to loosen from its shell.

2. Add the butternut and tomato. Cover and simmer for about 10 minutes, until the butternut is soft. Add the salt, Red Masala, turmeric and lemon juice, and gently beat the soupy mixture with a whisk.

3. Prepare the pan spices. Heat the oil in a small saucepan. Add the cumin seeds, asafoetida, curry leaves and red chilli shell. Stir once, allow the spices to sizzle for about 20 seconds, then add directly to the simmering moong (the spices will hiss and splutter as they are poured in). 'Clean' the saucepan with 1 Tbsp water and a little simmering moong, scraping up any remaining spices, and pour this into the pot.

4. Cover and continue simmering for 5–10 minutes, until the desired thickness is reached. Sprinkle with the fresh coriander and remove from the heat.

Whole moong should be soupy but not watery. Serve hot in soup bowls with blobs of ghee (optional), and fresh hot 'Classic Roti' (p. 147).

Hints and variations

For quicker cooking, soak the moong in water overnight. And for an extra tasty (and rich!) treat, add a little finely chopped onion and 2 Tbsp fresh cream to the pan spices in step 3. Stir well and braise until the onion is thoroughly cooked, then proceed as normal. Note also that if butternut is not available, you may use gem squash or pumpkin instead.

Delicious 'Dry' Dhal

Preparation time: 10 minutes Soaking time: 1 hour Cooking time: 15 minutes Serves 4
Red Masala, Three-spice Masala, Warm Masala

This dhal is made from hulled moong (mung beans). It is a richly flavoursome dish that can be prepared in a jiffy. Soak the dhal in the morning and whip it up in under half an hour for lunch.

1 cup moong dhal (hulled whole moong)
½ tsp salt
⅛ tsp turmeric
½ tsp Three-spice Masala
¾ tsp Warm Masala
pinch asafoetida
1½ Tbsp oil
½ finely chopped onion
½ tsp Red Masala
¾ cup water
1 heaped Tbsp finely chopped fresh coriander
1 heaped Tbsp finely chopped spring onions

TO GARNISH
2 heaped Tbsp finely chopped fresh coriander

1. Sort the dhal for discoloured and substandard pieces, rinse and drain. Soak in water for 1 hour, until swollen and succulent, then drain well.

2. Heat a deep, medium-sized pot on low. When the base of the pot is warm, add the dhal. Stir in the salt, turmeric, Three-spice and Warm Masalas and asafoetida. Add the oil, onion and Red Masala, and stir in thoroughly.

3. Add the water and bring to a rapid simmer. Reduce the heat and stir in the coriander and spring onions. Partially cover and simmer for 10 minutes, stirring occasionally. Guard against over-boiling at first, and scorching towards the end. Add water by the quarter cupful if necessary to finish the cooking. The water should be completely cooked away before serving.

The dhal should be a deep lemon yellow colour and slightly mushy. Sprinkle with fresh coriander and serve warm, on its own or with 'Classic Roti' (p. 147) and 'Carrot Atchar' (p. 33).

Butternut Dhal

Preparation time: 10 minutes Cooking time: 1½ hours Serves 6
Red Masala

There is an Indian saying that goes, 'If your dhal is right, then your day is right'. This recipe is sure to make your day right! The bright orange dhal is as warming as it looks, and indescribably tasty. One of its secret delights is to drink it straight from a mug, allowing the glow to spread inside you. Sheer bliss!

1 cup oil (toovar) dhal

3½ cups water

50 g or about ½ cup finely diced butternut

1 finely chopped tomato

1 finely diced carrot (optional)

¼ cup finely diced pineapple (optional)

1½ tsp salt

½ tsp Red Masala

¼ tsp turmeric

4½ tsp sugar

4½ Tbsp lemon juice

1 Tbsp oil

6–8 torn or lightly crushed curry leaves
(fresh or dried)

2 Tbsp finely chopped fresh coriander

PAN SPICES

1 dried red chilli shell, de-seeded (optional)

½ tsp mustard seeds

½ tsp cumin seeds

¼ tsp fenugreek seeds

pinch asafoetida

TO GARNISH

2 heaped Tbsp finely chopped fresh coriander

1. Soak the dhal in a bowl of water for 1 minute and drain in a colander. Rinse the dhal under a tap and drain thoroughly.

2. Bring 3 cups of water to the boil in a large pot. Add the dhal and reduce the heat. Partially cover and simmer for 20 minutes.

3. Add the butternut, tomato, carrot and pineapple and stir in well. Partially cover and simmer until all the vegetables are cooked through.

4. Pour the dhal mixture into a liquidiser. Blend until completely smooth. Return it to the pot and place on medium-low heat. Add the salt, Red Masala, turmeric, sugar and lemon juice. Partially cover and continue simmering.

5. Meanwhile, heat the oil in a small saucepan and add the dried chilli shell. When the oil is hot, add the mustard, cumin and fenugreek seeds, stir and allow to sizzle for about 20 seconds. Add the asafoetida, stir once, then pour the pan spices directly into the simmering dhal (it will hiss and splutter). 'Clean' the saucepan with 1 Tbsp water and a little dhal, and pour this into the pot.

6. Stir in the curry leaves, followed by the coriander. Add ½ cup water, raise the heat and bring to the boil, stirring well. Once the dhal reaches boiling point, the dish is done. Remove the pot from the heat and cover to keep warm.

Garnish with fresh coriander. The dhal should be an intense orange and quite thick. Serve with 'Plain Rice' (p. 143), or on its own as a thick soup.

Hints and variations
Other ingredients that work well with this dhal are diced pumpkin and grated apple. Adjust its colour and strength at any stage with a dash of chilli powder, or, if it's too strong, temper it with half a grated tomato.

Sweet & Sour Dhal

Preparation time: 15 minutes Soaking time: 1–2 hours Cooking time: 25 minutes Serves 2
Green Masala

Your kitchen will fill with a pleasant roasted aroma when you prepare this dish – and your mouth with pure sweet-sour pleasure with every bite!

1 cup soaked chickpea (gram) dhal
1 Tbsp oil
1½ cups freshly boiled water
½ tsp salt
⅛ tsp turmeric
1 tsp Green Masala
2 Tbsp lemon juice
6–7 torn or lightly crushed curry leaves
(fresh or dry)
1½ tsp sugar
1 heaped Tbsp finely chopped fresh coriander

PAN SPICE
½ tsp mustard seeds

TO GARNISH
1 heaped Tbsp finely chopped fresh coriander

1. Sort the chickpea dhal, rinse under a tap and drain, then soak in warm water for a minimum of 1 hour (preferably two) and drain again. The dhal should be very tender. Mince it in a food processor on low speed to a coarse mash.

2. Heat the oil in a wide pot. When hot, add the mustard seeds, stir and allow to sizzle for about 20 seconds. Reduce the heat to low, then add the minced dhal. Braise for 5 minutes, stirring continuously, until it releases a pleasant, roasted aroma. It will stick to the bottom of the pan: reincorporate the stickings before they scorch.

3. Stir in the freshly boiled water. Cover and simmer for 15 minutes, stirring occasionally. The dhal will absorb the water and become a thick mush. Add the salt, turmeric and Green Masala, stir, and then the lemon juice, curry leaves and sugar. Adjust for sweetness/ sourness with extra sugar/lemon juice. Cover and steam for 7–10 minutes, stirring every 2 minutes. Stir in the coriander, then remove from the heat.

Garnish with fresh coriander. Serve warm on its own or with 'Quick Coriander Chutney' (p. 24).

Hints and variations
When sorting dhal, the green peas are OK, the black or brown ones aren't.

Speckled Sugar Beans

Preparation time: 10 minutes Cooking time: 2½ hours Serves 4
Red Masala, Three-spice Masala, Warm Masala

Three masalas combine to make an irresistibly rich gravy – perfect food for a chilly winter evening.

1½ cups 'white' speckled sugar beans
1 finely chopped tomato
2 Tbsp oil
½ finely chopped onion
2 tsp salt
1½ tsp Red Masala
1 tsp turmeric
½ tsp Three-spice Masala
6–7 torn or lightly crushed curry leaves
(fresh or dried)
water for simmering
2 tsp sugar

PAN SPICES
3 whole cloves
6–7 cinnamon stick pieces

TO GARNISH
1 tsp Warm Masala
2 Tbsp finely chopped fresh coriander

1. Rinse the sugar beans under a tap and drain. Place in a medium-sized pot, cover with water and bring to the boil on high. Reduce the heat, cover and simmer for about 2 hours, until the beans are very tender. Add water if necessary: the sugar beans should be covered with water at all times.

2. Add the tomato, cover and continue to simmer for 5 minutes. Meanwhile, prepare the pan spices. Heat the oil in a small saucepan. When hot, add the cloves and cinnamon, stir well, then reduce the heat. Add the onion, cover and braise for 3–5 minutes, stirring occasionally, until golden brown and cooked through. Remove the saucepan from the heat.

3. Add the salt, Red Masala, turmeric, Three-spice Masala and curry leaves to the sugar beans, stirring well. Add the braised onion and pan spices, plus ½ cup water or more, depending on the desired amount of gravy. Raise the heat, bring the sugar beans to the boil, then reduce the heat, cover and simmer for 2–3 minutes. Sprinkle the sugar over the sugar beans, then remove the pot from the heat.

Garnish with Warm Masala, followed by fresh coriander. Serve warm with fresh 'Classic Roti' (p. 147) or 'Plain Rice' (p. 143).

Hints and variations
When selecting sugar beans, choose the highest grade available. The beans should be large, whole, smooth and mostly white, with reddish speckles. For presentation, you can add a few slices of raw onion to each bowl served. Butter beans – or other large, meaty beans – make a good substitute for sugar beans.

Chickpea and Potato Curry

Preparation time: 10 minutes Cooking time: 35 minutes Serves 2

Red Masala, Three-spice Masala, Warm Masala

Here is the quickest curry of them all, and one of the most delicious, using whole chickpeas from a tin.

2 Tbsp oil

¼ finely chopped onion

1 finely chopped tomato

1 tsp salt

½ tsp Red Masala

¼ tsp turmeric

½ tsp Three-spice Masala

7–10 torn or lightly crushed curry leaves (fresh or dry)

2 potatoes, peeled and sliced into medium pieces

1 cup water

400 g tinned chickpeas, drained

splash lemon juice

½ tsp Warm Masala

¼ tsp sugar (optional)

PAN SPICES

¼ tsp mustard seeds

3–4 cinnamon stick pieces

TO GARNISH

2 heaped Tbsp finely chopped fresh coriander

1. Heat the oil in a medium-sized pot on medium-high. When hot, add the mustard seeds and cinnamon sticks, stir and allow to sizzle for about 20 seconds. Add the onion, cover and braise for 3–5 minutes until golden brown and cooked through, stirring occasionally.

2. Reduce the heat. Add the tomato, salt, Red Masala, turmeric, Three-spice Masala and curry leaves, and stir in well. Cover and cook until the tomato is well-amalgamated with the onion. Add the potatoes and ½ cup water and stir. Cover and simmer for 15–20 minutes, until the potatoes are soft. Add water by the half-cupful if necessary to prevent scorching.

3. Add the chickpeas, lemon juice, Warm Masala and ½ cup water. Cover and simmer for a final 10–15 minutes, until the gravy is thick.

Sprinkle the sugar (optional) over the dish. Garnish with fresh coriander. Serve with 'Plain Rice' (p. 143).

Spicy Green Beans and Potatoes

Preparation time: 10 minutes Cooking time: 30 minutes Serves 4
Red Masala, Three-spice Masala

Like the next two recipes, this is a classic 'dry' vegetable curry.

2 Tbsp oil
¼ finely chopped onion
½ tsp salt
½ tsp Red Masala
½ tsp turmeric
½ tsp Three-spice Masala
150 g (about 1½ cups)
halved and thinly sliced green beans
1 peeled potato, sliced into small pieces
1 cup water
½ grated tomato
½ tsp sugar (optional)

PAN SPICES
¼ tsp tynol (ajowan)
pinch asafoetida

1. Heat the oil in a small pot on medium-high. When hot, add the tynol and asafoetida, stir and allow to sizzle for about 20 seconds. Add the onion, cover and braise for 3–5 minutes until golden brown and cooked through.

2. Add the salt and Red Masala, then the turmeric and Three-spice Masala. Add the beans and potato and gently stir through the spices. Reduce the heat, add ¼ cup water, stir and cover. Steam for 5–7 minutes, until the water has almost completely evaporated. Add ½ cup water, cover and steam until the vegetables are nearly cooked through.

3. Spoon the tomato over the dish, add the final ¼ cup water and stir in gently. Cover and steam until the water has completely evaporated, about 5–7 minutes.

Sprinkle with sugar and a pinch of salt if desired. Serve warm with 'Plain Rice' (p. 143) or as a side dish with dhals or meat curries.

Hints and variations

To test a batch of raw green beans for freshness and succulence, snap a bean in half: if it bends significantly before it breaks, it's old and tough!

Spicy Cabbage

Preparation time: 10 minutes Cooking time: 35 minutes Serves 2–4
Red Masala, Three-spice Masala

Plain cabbage comes to life in this delicious, nutritious 'dry' vegetable curry.

500 g green cabbage (about ¼ head)
2 Tbsp oil
½ finely chopped onion
1 tsp salt
½ tsp Red Masala
½ tsp turmeric
1 tsp Three-spice Masala
½ grated tomato (note: grate the tomato only when required in step 3)
¼ tsp sugar (optional)

PAN SPICES
½ tsp mustard seeds
¼ tsp fenugreek seeds
pinch asafoetida

1. Remove the cabbage's outer leaves and its thick, white base stem. Remove any thick central 'veins' and shred the cabbage into stubby ribbons.

2. Heat the oil in a medium-sized pot on medium-high. When hot, add the pan spices, stir and allow to sizzle for about 20 seconds. Reduce the heat, add the onion, cover and braise for 3–5 minutes until golden brown and cooked through, stirring occasionally.

3. Add the salt, Red Masala, turmeric and Three-spice Masala, stirring well. Add the cabbage, stir through the spices thoroughly, and cover. Cook for 15 minutes, stirring every 3–5 minutes to prevent scorching.

4. Grate the tomato over the cabbage and gently stir in. Cover and steam for 15 minutes, until the cabbage is translucent and tender. Stir occasionally. Remove the cover for a final few minutes to allow the remaining juices to evaporate. The cabbage is done when it no longer leaves streaks when stirred.

Sprinkle with sugar. Serve warm as a side dish to accompany most curries.

Hints and variations

One whole baby cabbage is an excellent replacement for the quarter head called for here: simply reduce the cooking time by 5–10 minutes. You may add 50 g finely diced carrots to the cabbage, or reverse the cabbage/carrot proportions for a vibrant orange variation.

Spicy Cauliflower

Preparation time: 10 minutes Cooking time: 25 minutes Serves 4
Red Masala, Three-spice Masala

A medley of vegetables glisten like jewels in this classic 'dry' curry.

200 g cauliflower (about ¼ head),
broken up into small florets
50 g halved and thinly sliced green beans
(optional)
2 Tbsp oil
¼ finely chopped onion
¾ tsp salt
½ tsp Red Masala
¼ tsp turmeric
½ tsp Three-spice Masala
4 Tbsp water
50 g or about ½ cup diced butternut
½ finely chopped tomato
¼ cup peas, fresh or frozen (optional)
¼ tsp sugar (optional)

PAN SPICES
½ tsp mustard seeds
½ tsp cumin seeds
pinch asafoetida

1. Mix the cauliflower florets and green beans together in a bowl. Heat the oil in a small pot. When hot, add the mustard and cumin seeds and the asafoetida, stir and allow to sizzle for about 20 seconds. Add the onion, cover and braise for 3–5 minutes until golden brown and thoroughly cooked, stirring occasionally.

2. Reduce the heat. Add the salt, Red Masala, turmeric and Three-spice Masala, stirring well. Add the cauliflower and green beans and stir gently through the spices. Add 2 Tbsp water, cover and steam for 4–5 minutes, until the vegetables are tender-crisp.

3. Add the butternut and stir in gently, then cover and steam for 3 minutes. Sprinkle the tomato and peas over the vegetables, add 2 Tbsp water, cover and steam for a further 20 minutes, stirring gently every few minutes, until all the vegetables are thoroughly cooked. Add water by the Tbsp if necessary to prevent sticking, not to aid cooking.

Sprinkle with the sugar (optional). Serve to accompany any dish, or as a main dish with 'Plain Rice' (p. 143) or 'Classic Roti' (p. 147).

Hints and variations
Carrots make a good substitute for the butternut.

Peas in the Pod

Preparation time: 10 minutes Cooking time: 35 minutes Serves 2–4
Red Masala, Three-spice Masala

When peas in the pod are in season, snap them up for this recipe! It's a true delicacy which makes for a delicious treat, and an especially fun starter (see eating instructions below).

400 g peas in the pod
2½ Tbsp oil
¼ finely chopped onion
½ tsp Red Masala
2 peeled potatoes, sliced into large pieces
½ tsp salt
½ tsp turmeric
100 g (about 1 cup) halved and thinly sliced green beans
¼ cup water
7–10 torn or lightly crushed curry leaves (fresh or dry)
½ tsp Three-spice Masala
¼ tsp sugar (optional)

PAN SPICE
½ tsp tynol (ajowan)

1. Trim the pea pods of excessively long stems (leaving the stem nibs for ease of eating), rinse and drain. Heat the oil in a wide pot on medium-high. When hot, add the tynol and allow to sizzle for about 20 seconds. Add the onion, cover and braise for 3–5 minutes, until golden brown and thoroughly cooked, stirring occasionally. Add the Red Masala, stir, and reduce the heat. Add the potatoes and pea pods, then the salt and turmeric, and stir to distribute the turmeric's colour. Cover and cook for 5 minutes. Add water by the Tbsp if necessary to prevent scorching.

2. Stir the green beans in carefully. Cover and cook for 10 minutes, stirring every few minutes, adding water by the Tbsp if necessary. Do not over-disturb the pea pods, or they will break open.

3. Add the water, curry leaves and Three-spice Masala. Cover and steam until the water has completely evaporated, 15–20 minutes. The dish is ready when the potatoes are cooked and the pods have a slightly 'furry' texture.

Sprinkle with sugar (optional). Serve warm with 'Plain Rice' (p. 143). Eat the pea pods by pinching the stem nib between thumb and forefinger, placing the pod in your mouth and gently pulling it through your front teeth. The peas will pop out of the pod, and the pod's succulent, furry skin will scrape off on your teeth. Messy and delicious!

Hints and variations
Unfortunately, mangetout won't do as a substitute for peas in the pod: they're too thin and flimsy.

Variation: substitute the green beans and potato with thick carrot sticks and quartered sweet potatoes.

Fried Aubergine Medallions

Preparation time: 10 minutes Cooking time: 15–20 minutes Serves 4

Red Masala, Three-spice Masala, Warm Masala

There's nothing more delectable than aubergine spiced with masala straight from the pan.

½ medium aubergine (brinjal)
½ tsp salt
½ tsp Red Masala
¼ tsp turmeric
½ tsp Three-spice Masala
¼ tsp Warm Masala
½ tsp paprika or chilli powder
½ Tbsp oil
oil for frying
cake (plain) flour for dipping
water for steaming

TO GARNISH
1 Tbsp finely chopped fresh coriander

1. Slice the aubergine evenly into medallions 1–2 cm thick, starting from the vine end of the plant. Sprinkle the medallions with a little salt and soak in cold water for about 10 minutes (the water will darken). Drain, rinse gently and pat dry. Scrape the medallions with the edge of a spoon to remove excess pips, but ignore those embedded in the flesh.

2. Mix the salt, Red Masala, turmeric, Three-spice Masala, Warm Masala, paprika or chilli powder and ½ Tbsp oil into a paste. Rub it gently into both sides of each medallion. Prepare to cook them immediately.

3. Pour enough oil into a medium-sized non-stick frying pan to cover the base thinly, and heat on medium. Prepare a wide bowl with a few Tbsp cake flour. When the oil is hot, press the medallions into the cake flour so that each side is lightly and evenly coated, then place as many as possible into the pan. Cover and fry for 4–5 minutes. Turn the medallions with a fork. The tops should be crispy and golden, not burnt. Sprinkle the pan with 2 Tbsp water, cover and fry for an additional 4–5 minutes. Remove the medallions and drain on kitchen paper. Add oil to the pan if necessary to complete the frying, but only in small amounts, lest the medallions overcook.

Sprinkle the medallions with coriander. They're best served hot, fresh out of the pan.

Hints and variations

Choose an aubergine that is young, dark, shiny and firm. If you plan to keep the medallions aside after frying, lay them out individually on kitchen paper and leave uncovered (covered or stacked medallions become soggy).

Moong (Mung Bean) Sprouts

Preparation time: 5 minutes Sprouting time: 3 days Cooking time: 1 hour Serves 4–6
Red Masala, Three-spice Masala, Warm Masala

Sprouts are among the most nutritious of foods, and preparing them with masala is a delicious twist. This recipe will serve as many as six, but halve or quarter it and you have a scrumptious snack.

1 Tbsp oil
1 finely chopped onion
1 tsp salt
1 tsp Red Masala
1 tsp turmeric
1 tsp Three-spice Masala
1 tsp Warm Masala
6–7 torn or lightly crushed curry leaves
(fresh or dry)
1 cup whole dry moong, soaked and sprouted,
or 5 cups moong sprouts
1¾ cups water

PAN SPICES
½ tsp cumin seeds
¼ tsp asafoetida

TO GARNISH
2 heaped Tbsp finely chopped fresh coriander

1. Heat the oil in a wide, deep pot on medium. When hot, add the cumin seeds and asafoetida. Stir and allow the spices to sizzle for about 20 seconds. Add the onion, cover and braise for 3–5 minutes until golden brown and cooked through, stirring occasionally. Stir in the salt, Red Masala and turmeric, then add the Three-spice Masala, Warm Masala and curry leaves. Add the sprouts and stir thoroughly through the spices.

2. Add the water, raise the heat, and cover. Bring to a rapid simmer, then reduce the heat. Steam the sprouts until thoroughly tender, about 40 minutes. Add water by the quarter cupful if necessary to prevent scorching. The dish is done when the sprouts are tender and the water has completely evaporated.

Garnish with coriander, turning it through the sprouts with a spoon. Serve with 'Plain Soft Puri' (p. 149).

Hints and variations

Make your own sprouts! Pour whole dry moong into a deep, narrow pot or bowl. Add 1 cup cold water to 2½ cups freshly boiled water, pour over the moong (the water should not be too hot – you should be able to touch it) and cover. Soak the moong for 8–12 hours, preferably overnight. Drain the water thoroughly, and cover the moong with a layer of porous paper, such as newspaper. Insulate with additional layers of paper and cover with a lid. Store the moong in a dark, warm place. Allow it to stand undisturbed for 2 days. (It will begin to sprout after about 12 hours.) The moong is ready for cooking when the sprout shoots are 1 cm long. Fill the pot with cold water, then drain the moong in a colander. The volume of the moong will have almost quintupled!

Masala Fried Potatoes

Preparation time: 5 minutes Cooking time: 25 minutes Serves 4
Red Masala

One word: 'Yum!' This is a favourite snack of adults and children alike. It's a stand-by, too, when you're in need of a quick side dish to complement a main course.

3 potatoes
5 Tbsp oil
1 tsp salt
1 tsp Red Masala
¼ tsp turmeric
5–6 torn or lightly crushed curry leaves
(fresh or dried)

PAN SPICES
½ tsp mustard seeds
⅛ tsp fenugreek seeds
½ tsp cumin seeds

TO GARNISH
2 heaped Tbsp finely chopped fresh coriander

1. Peel the potatoes, rinse, and slice into 1 cm cubes. Soak for 30 seconds in a bowl of water. Drain and dry on kitchen paper.

2. Heat the oil in a non-stick frying pan on high. When hot, add the mustard seeds, fenugreek, cumin seeds and salt. Stir once, then add the Red Masala and turmeric. Stir well and flash-fry for about 10 seconds.

3. Reduce the heat to medium. Add the potatoes and stir thoroughly. Cover and fry for 10 minutes, stirring every 2–3 minutes.

4. Add the curry leaves to the potatoes and stir. Cover and fry for an additional 10 minutes, until the potatoes are a dark golden colour and cooked through. Add oil if necessary to prevent scorching but do not overcook – the potatoes can become mushy.

Sprinkle with fresh coriander. Serve hot as a snack, or to complete these classic Indian combinations: 'Khari' (p. 32), 'Plain Rice' (p. 143) and 'Savoury Spinach' (p. 57); or 'Whole Moong (Mung Beans)' (p. 40) and 'Classic Roti' (p. 147).

Hints and variations
Potatoes generally use a lot of oil when frying, and individual spuds may differ in their requirements: add more oil by the Tbsp if necessary to complete your batch.

Savoury Spinach

Preparation time: 5 minutes Cooking time: 25 minutes Serves 4
Red Masala

This simple recipe is a classic side dish, often served alongside 'Khari' (p. 32), 'Plain Rice' (p.143) and 'Masala Fried Potatoes' (p. 56). Prepare it once and you may never serve spinach any other way again!

200 g (about 1 bunch) spinach
2 Tbsp oil
¾ finely chopped onion
1 tsp salt
¼ tsp Red Masala
½ tsp turmeric

PAN SPICES
½ tsp fenugreek seeds
½ tsp cumin seeds

1. Wash the spinach leaves thoroughly, remove the central stalks and coarsely shred.

2. Heat the oil in a wide pot, or deep frying pan with a lid, on medium-high. When hot, add the fenugreek and cumin seeds, stir once and allow to sizzle for about 20 seconds. Add the onion, cover and braise for 3–5 minutes until golden brown and cooked through.

3. Add the salt, Red Masala and turmeric and stir in well. Braise the spices in the onion for about 30 seconds. Add the shredded spinach, stirring continuously for 2–3 minutes, until all has been exposed to the heat. Reduce the heat, then cover. Cook the spinach for 10–12 minutes, stirring every 2 minutes. (It will shrink dramatically.) Remove the cover for a final 3–5 minutes of cooking.

The dish is done when excess water on the bottom of the pan has evaporated and the spinach no longer leaves wet streaks when moved with a spoon. Serve warm as a side dish with any Indian meal.

Hints and variations
The key to this dish's bulk and richness of flavour is the chopped onion: if you find yourself short of spinach leaves, increase the amount of onion. Note that it is especially important that both the onion and spinach are thoroughly cooked (softened) before serving.

Okra Curry

Preparation time: 10 minutes Cooking time: 25 minutes Serves 2
Red Masala, Three-spice Masala

Okra is highly nutritious and energy giving, and has a wonderful, almost nutty flavour. This curry may be served as a side dish, but is also excellent as an exotic main attraction!

250 g okra
2 Tbsp oil
½ finely chopped onion
¾ tsp salt
½ tsp Red Masala
½ tsp turmeric
½ tsp Three-spice Masala
1 peeled and diced potato
½ finely chopped tomato
½ tsp sugar (optional)

PAN SPICE
½ tsp fenugreek seeds

TO GARNISH
1 heaped Tbsp finely chopped fresh coriander

1. Rinse the okra, drain and pat dry with kitchen paper. Remove the stems and slice into star-shaped cross-sections about 1 cm thick.

2. Heat the oil in a medium-sized frying pan. When hot, add the fenugreek seeds, stir and allow to sizzle for about 20 seconds. Add the onion, cover and braise for 2–3 minutes, until on the verge of golden brown. Stir occasionally.

3. Reduce the heat. Add the salt, Red Masala, turmeric and Three-spice Masala, and stir well. Add the potatoes, stir and cover. Fry for 5 minutes, stirring occasionally.

4. Add the okra, cover and continue frying for about 5 minutes, until its gluey juices begin to burn away. Remove the cover, sprinkle with the finely chopped tomato, and gently turn through with a spoon. Fry, uncovered, for 4–5 minutes, until the last of the okra's sticky juices have burned away. Guard against overcooking, as the okra will become soggy.

Sprinkle with sugar (optional) and garnish with fresh coriander. Serve with 'Classic Roti' (p. 147) as a scrumptious main dish.

Hints and variations
When selecting okra, choose a thin, short sample and press your thumbnail into its skin. The skin should 'pop' and yield without much pressure, and the flesh should be moist. Avoid large or thick okra, and okra with tough skin. Okra complements meat dishes particularly well, for instance 'Lamb Curry' (p. 93).

Khaman

Preparation time: 10 minutes Cooking time: 12–15 minutes Serves 6
Green Masala

Khaman (the 'kh' is pronounced like a raspy 'h') is a delicious conveyor of dainty flavours and fragrances, and makes an excellent appetiser. Steamed on the stove-top, tangy with buttermilk and Green Masala, drizzled with an uncommonly fine mixture of seasonings – this dish might be called a 'rarity' were it not for the fact that you can prepare it in half an hour!

DOUGH
½ tsp salt
½ tsp Green Masala
⅛ tsp turmeric
1 Tbsp oil
1 cup semolina
¾ cup plain yoghurt or buttermilk
1 tsp lemon juice (optional if using buttermilk)
¼ cup water
1 tsp baking powder
pinch bicarbonate of soda
water for steaming
oil for greasing

DRESSING
2 Tbsp oil
8–10 torn or lightly crushed curry leaves
(fresh or dried)
2 tsp mustard seeds
1 tsp sesame seeds
2 tsp shredded coconut (optional)

TO GARNISH
1 heaped Tbsp finely chopped fresh coriander

1. Prepare the dough. Mix the salt, Green Masala, turmeric and oil in a wide bowl. Add the semolina and stir well. Add the yoghurt or buttermilk, lemon juice and water, and mix thoroughly. The dough should be sticky and not at all stiff. Add 2 Tbsp extra water if necessary to achieve this consistency, especially when using yoghurt instead of buttermilk. Cover the dough and leave it to stand for 5 minutes.

2. Bring 2 cm water to a simmer in a wide, deep pot. Meanwhile, add the baking powder and bicarbonate of soda to the dough and mix in well. Spoon the dough into a round, greased cake tin (17 cm in diameter). When the water is simmering, place a flattened steaming trivet in the pot and the dough-filled cake tin on top of it. Cover the pot and steam the dough undisturbed for 10–12 minutes. Remove the cover and test with a fork: if it comes out clean, the khaman's done. Remove the cake tin from the pot.

3. Prepare the dressing. Heat the oil in a small pot. When hot, add the curry leaves and mustard and sesame seeds, stir, and allow to sizzle for about 20 seconds. Add the shredded coconut, and stir once. Drizzle over the cooling khaman immediately.

4. Garnish with coriander, cut the khaman into square or diamond shapes and serve hot with 'Quick Coriander Chutney' (p. 24).

Hints and variations
Stir in 1 heaped Tbsp fresh, finely chopped fenugreek during step 1 for a slightly more savoury variation.

Sweetcorn Fritters

Preparation time: 10 minutes Cooking time: 25 minutes Serves 6–8 Yields 25–30
Green Masala

This is fabulous, effortless finger food. Simply mix and fry. The Green Masala ensures an irresistibly piquant flavour – make sure everyone gets at least one!

1 cup cake (plain) flour
½ tsp baking powder
450 g (1 tin) cream-style sweetcorn kernels
1 egg
1 tsp Green Masala
½ tsp salt
⅛ tsp turmeric
½ tsp chilli powder
1 tsp sugar
1 heaped Tbsp finely chopped fresh coriander
150 g (about 1 medium)
finely diced green pepper, de-seeded
3 Tbsp oil

1. Sift the flour into a wide mixing bowl, then add the baking powder and stir. Add the sweetcorn, egg and Green Masala and stir in well. Add the salt, turmeric, chilli powder, sugar, fresh coriander and green pepper, mixing thoroughly. A thin but well-bound batter should result, which drops off a spoon easily in one 'blob'.

2. Heat the oil in a medium non-stick frying pan. Ensure that the oil is spread thinly over the base. When hot, spoon the batter into the pan with a dinner or soup spoon, allowing each spoonful to drop from a height of 10–15 cm, so that it flattens somewhat when it drops into the pan. Fry for about 45 seconds per side, flipping three times with a fork, for a total cooking time of 3–4 minutes, until the fritters are an even dark golden brown. Add more oil by the Tbsp if required to complete the frying.

Serve hot out of the pan.

Fried Courgette Cakes

Preparation time: 15 minutes Cooking time: 20 minutes Serves 4–6 Yields 25
Red Masala, Three-spice Masala

These golden-yellow cakes taste as good as they look. Courgette – also known as baby marrow – is a splendidly versatile food, and here the Three-spice Masala imparts a rich seasoning to its sweet flesh.

300 g courgettes
¼ cup chickpea (gram) dhal flour
¼ cup cake (plain) flour
¼ cup maize meal
¼ tsp baking powder
1½ tsp salt
½ tsp Red Masala
½ tsp turmeric
1½ tsp Three-spice Masala
½ tsp coarsely crushed fennel seeds
1 tsp oil
1 tsp sugar
1 heaped Tbsp finely chopped fresh coriander
½ tsp chilli powder (optional)
4 Tbsp oil for frying

1. Peel the courgette, removing dry or hard flesh, or any that is tinged with the colour of the rind. Scoop out the seeds and inner webbing. Grate the flesh into a wide bowl.

2. Prepare the batter by mixing together the grated courgette, the flours, maize meal and baking powder. Work the courgette through vigorously, 'mashing' it with your hands. Add the salt, Red Masala, turmeric, Three-spice Masala and crushed fennel and mix thoroughly. Add the 1 tsp oil, sugar, fresh coriander and chilli powder. 'Knead' the mixture into a stiff, well-bound batter.

3. Shape the batter into about 25 small patties, each 5 cm in diameter. Heat 4 Tbsp oil in a small frying pan on medium-high. When hot, place 4–5 patties in at a time. Fry for about 1 minute per side, flipping at least three times with a fork, for a total cooking time of about 4 minutes, until the cakes are a dark golden yellow and somewhat crispy. Open one to test if it is done: it should steam and have a soft, but not gooey, centre. Add more oil to the pan if necessary to complete the frying.

Drain the cakes on kitchen paper. Serve hot as a starter or finger food.

Hints and variations

To test a courgette for freshness, select a medium-sized one that has a dark, shiny skin. Press your thumbnail gently into the rind: if it sinks in easily, it's fresh.

Spinach Parcels

Preparation time: 30 minutes Cooking time: 35–40 minutes Serves 4–6
Red Masala, Three-spice Masala, Warm Masala

Spinach and its broad-leafed cognates are important elements in Indian cuisine, put to a variety of daily uses. In our opinion, nothing tops this dish for sheer spinach ingenuity! The green vegetable is rolled out and used almost like pastry dough to create a cross between a hearty, savoury pie and a delectable steamed salad. Tightly-wrapped spinach parcels make great 'on-the-go' food, but also provide a tempting gourmet accent to any main fare, especially when presented in thin slices.

18 (about 300 g) broad spinach leaves
1½ cups maize meal
1 cup cake (plain) flour
¾ cup chickpea dhal (gram) flour
2 tsp salt
¾ tsp turmeric
2 tsp Three-spice Masala
½ tsp Warm Masala
1½ Tbsp sugar
½ tsp paprika
½ tsp tynol (ajowan) (optional)
1 Tbsp oil
½ tsp sesame seeds
1½ tsp Red Masala
6 Tbsp white vinegar
1 Tbsp lemon juice
¾ cup water
oil for frying
water for steaming

1. When selecting spinach, choose a broad-leaved, thin-stalked bunch unblighted by insects, preferably from the non-refrigerated part of the produce section. (Slightly wilted leaves make for easier folding. Do not keep spinach intended for this recipe in your fridge.)

2. Rinse the leaves and trim the centre stalks at the base. Pat dry with kitchen paper. Roll out the leaves one by one with a rolling pin, going over each leaf twice (once up, once down), flattening the stalk, ends and tips so that the leaf is mostly flat.

3. Prepare the batter. Mix the maize meal and flours in a wide bowl. Add the salt, turmeric, Three-spice Masala, Warm Masala, sugar, paprika and tynol, and mix well. Add 1 Tbsp oil, the sesame seeds and Red Masala, and press vigorously through the flour with the back of a spoon, until small clumps form. Add the vinegar and lemon juice and stir in well. Mix in the water to finish. The batter should be smooth and thick, flowing slowly in the direction it is tipped.

Continued on p. 66

4. Make the parcels. Select three spinach leaves of roughly the same size. Place the first leaf with its 'pointy' side facing away from you, and spread a thin layer of batter on it with your hands, rubbing from the centre stalk outwards, along the grain of the leaf's veins. Place the second leaf, pointing in the same direction, partly over the first leaf, so that the left half of the second leaf overlaps the right half of the first. Spread the second leaf with batter. Place the third leaf, 'pointy' side facing toward you, over the first two leaves, so that its broad end covers the gap left by the first two, and the 'point' reaches down three-quarters of the length of the other leaves.

5. Fold the left half of the first leaf to the centre of the third leaf. Spread the shiny side of the first leaf with a thin layer of batter. Fold the right half of the second leaf to the centre of the third leaf, and spread it with batter. Now fold this three-leaf rectangle into a square: starting at the bottom of the rectangle, fold over about a quarter of the rectangle's length. Spread the shiny side with batter. Repeat twice, then seal the final fold with batter. The spinach parcel is done. Prepare 5 more parcels with the remaining spinach leaves.

6. Heat 1½ Tbsp oil in a wide non-stick frying pan. When hot, place 2–3 parcels in the pan, cover and cook for 3 minutes (the water in the spinach will steam the parcels). Turn them, adding 1 Tbsp water to the pan. Cover and steam for an additional 3 minutes. Turn twice more, adding 1 Tbsp water with each turning, for a total cooking time of 12–15 minutes. The parcels will turn yellow-green, and will brown slightly. They are done when an inserted blade comes out clean. Add a fresh 1½ Tbsp of oil for each round of frying.

Serve the parcels hot or cold, cut in half or sliced thinly.

Hints and variations
Add 2 Tbsp shredded coconut and 1 Tbsp crushed, roasted peanuts for extra crunch.

Chickpea Dhal Meatballs

Preparation time: 45 minutes Soaking time: 4–12 hours Cooking time: 1 hour Serves 4–6 Yields 30
Red Masala, Three-spice Masala, Warm Masala

This is one of the supreme vegetarian curries, a two-part, three-masala wonder. The mouthwatering 'meatballs' are simmered in a delicately flavoured gravy for an effect that's almost impossibly delicious.

MEATBALLS
1 cup chickpea (gram) dhal
2 fresh green chillies
2 cloves garlic
10 g (1 small piece) peeled fresh ginger
2 heaped Tbsp very finely chopped fresh coriander or fenugreek
1½ tsp salt
1½ tsp Red Masala
½ tsp turmeric
1½ tsp Three-spice Masala
2½ tsp oil
1 tsp cake (plain) flour
oil for frying

GRAVY
4 Tbsp oil
½ finely chopped onion
1 tsp salt
½ tsp Red Masala
½ tsp turmeric
1½ tsp Three-spice Masala
4 cups water
2 peeled potatoes, sliced into medium pieces
2 finely chopped tomatoes

PAN SPICES
3 cardamom pods
3–4 cinnamon stick pieces
3 whole cloves

TO GARNISH
½ tsp Warm Masala
2 heaped Tbsp finely chopped fresh coriander

1. Sort the dhal, pour it into a bowl and cover with cold water. Soak overnight, or for a minimum of 4 hours. It will expand to twice its original volume. Drain well.

2. Coarsely chop the fresh green chillies and garlic and finely chop the ginger. Place these ingredients with the dhal in a food processor and mince on low speed, pausing to stir if necessary, until the mixture is very fine and smooth. Pour the minced dhal into a bowl, add the fresh coriander or fenugreek and mix in thoroughly.

3. Prepare the 'meatball' dough by mixing the salt, Red Masala, turmeric, Three-spice Masala and 2½ tsp oil with the minced dhal. Add the cake flour and stir in thoroughly. Working with about 1 Tbsp at a time, roll the mixture between your palms into small, egg-shaped balls (about 30). Reserve on a tray or dish.

4. Heat the oil to a depth of 0.5 cm in a medium-sized frying pan. When hot, add as many balls as possible

to the pan. Fry them, uncovered, for about 1 minute, then turn with a fork. Fry for a further 5 minutes, then turn again and fry 1 minute more. Remove the balls from the pan and drain on kitchen paper. They should be well-browned and crispy, with a reddish hue. Note: if two batches are required to complete the frying, discard the oil after the first batch and start again with fresh oil, otherwise bits of dhal will burn and the curry will take on a burnt flavour.

5. Prepare the gravy. Heat the oil in a wide pot on medium. Add the cardamom, cinnamon and cloves and allow to sizzle for about 1 minute. Add the onion, cover and braise for 3–5 minutes until golden brown and cooked through, stirring occasionally. Add the salt, Red Masala, turmeric and Three-spice Masala and stir well. Add the fried chickpea balls, then 3 cups of water and the potatoes. Raise the heat, bring the gravy to the boil, then simmer, covered, for about 10 minutes, until the balls are soft. Note that they should remain almost entirely covered in gravy throughout this step. Add water by the quarter cupful if necessary.

6. Spoon the tomatoes into the pot, then add 1 cup water and stir gently, careful not to break up the chickpea balls. Cover and simmer for 15 minutes, until the potatoes are thoroughly cooked.

Garnish with Warm Masala and fresh coriander, and serve warm with 'Classic Roti' (p. 147), 'Plain Soft Puri' (p. 149) or 'Plain Rice' (p. 143).

Hints and variations
If you prefer a thicker gravy, break up one or two of the chickpea meatballs during the simmering in step 5. You may also add 50 g grated butternut with the potatoes: this not only thickens the gravy, but lightens and sweetens the dish.

Indian 'Ravioli'

Preparation time: 45 minutes Cooking time: 40 minutes Serves 4
Green Masala, Red Masala, Three-spice Masala, Warm Masala

Pasta purists will immediately point out that, strictly speaking, this is not ravioli: there's no filling for the dough! And yet, the delectable pieces of pasta in this dish have the same shape and gorgeous 'slipperiness' of Italian ravioli, and the light green sauce is just as rich and zesty as its marinara counterpart. This recipe, which calls for all four masalas, is gourmet vegetarian cooking at its finest.

PASTA
1½ cups cake (plain) flour
¼ cup chickpea (gram) dhal flour
¾ cup maize meal
1 tsp salt
¾ tsp turmeric
1 tsp sesame seeds
1 tsp Green Masala
¼ tsp tynol (ajowan)
1 Tbsp oil
½ cup water
flour for dusting

SAUCE
1 Tbsp oil
50 g halved and thinly sliced green beans
1 tsp salt
¾ tsp Red Masala
¼ tsp turmeric
¼ tsp Three-spice Masala
3 cups water, room temperature
100 g peas (fresh or frozen)
7–10 torn or lightly crushed curry leaves
2 cups freshly boiled water

PAN SPICE
¼ tsp tynol (ajowan)

TO GARNISH
½ tsp Warm Masala
2 Tbsp finely chopped fresh coriander

1. Prepare the pasta. Mix the cake flour, dhal flour and maize meal with the salt, turmeric and sesame seeds. Add the Green Masala, tynol and oil, pressing them through the flour with the back of a spoon, until a dry dough results.

2. Add ½ cup water to the dough by the Tbsp, working each one in thoroughly, until the dough is slightly moist but still very stiff. Knead it for about 2 minutes, then shape it into a large ball.

3. Separate the dough ball into six equal pieces, then shape these into balls. Dust a rolling board with flour, press each ball flat between your palms, roll them out into 20 cm discs. (For easier rolling, first roll

them out to 10 cm discs, then reserve covered with a slightly damp cloth. After 10 minutes, complete the rolling.) Re-dust the board in-between balls. Lay out the discs of dough as they are rolled, and cover with a damp cloth.

4. Cut the dough discs with a pastry cutter into eight strips of equal width, then make eight equal cuts at a 90° angle, creating dough squares. Gently tear the squares apart, lay them out and cover with the damp cloth.

5. Prepare the sauce. Heat the oil in a wide pot. When hot, add the tynol and allow to sizzle for about 20 seconds. Reduce the heat, and add the green beans, salt, Red Masala, turmeric and Three-spice Masala, stirring well. Add ¼ cup water at room temperature. Cover the pot and steam for 5 minutes. Add the peas and curry leaves, cover and steam for an additional 5 minutes.

6. Add the freshly boiled water, stir and reduce the heat to low. Add the dough squares one at a time, gently agitating the pot to prevent sticking. As the pot fills up with pasta, stir it carefully with a wooden spoon. It will seem to become over-full: gently press the pasta pieces down into the sauce with the back of a spoon. After about half the pieces have been added, add 1¼ cups water at room temperature, and continue adding the remaining squares one at a time. Spoon the gravy over the top layers of the pasta, and disturb the bottom layers periodically, bringing these pieces to the top. (Some sticking is inevitable.)

7. Once all the pasta is in the pot, add 1½ cups water at room temperature. Raise the heat, cover, and simmer for 10 minutes, adding water by the quarter cupful for more gravy if desired.

Garnish with Warm Masala and fresh coriander. Serve hot.

Hints and variations

The maize meal in the pasta recipe can be replaced with rice flour. For a sweeter gravy, grate ½ tomato into the pot at the beginning of step 6. For a more piquant gravy, add ½ Tbsp lemon juice at the beginning of step 7. Note that the dough squares keep well in the deep freeze.

Poppy Seed Curry

Preparation time: 15 minutes Soaking time: 30 minutes Cooking time: 45 minutes Serves 2–4
Red Masala, Green Masala, Warm Masala

This is an unusual gourmet dish that perfectly replaces soup on a three-course Indian menu and delivers extravagantly on its implicit promise of rare, rich satisfaction.

½ cup white poppy seeds
2½ Tbsp oil
1 finely chopped onion
½ tsp Red Masala
½ tsp Green Masala
7–10 torn or lightly crushed
curry leaves (fresh or dry)
½ tsp salt
½ tsp turmeric
½ cup water
½ diced green pepper
4 heaped Tbsp finely chopped fresh fenugreek

PAN SPICE
¼ tsp fenugreek seeds

TO GARNISH
½ tsp Warm Masala
1 heaped Tbsp fresh coriander

1. Sort the poppy seeds on a white plate, removing black particles and chaff. Grind in three batches in a coffee/spice grinder until fine and powdery (some seeds will remain whole). Soak the ground seeds in water for a minimum of 30 minutes. Do not drain.

2. Heat the oil in a medium-sized pot on medium-high. When hot, add the fenugreek seeds, stir and allow to sizzle for about 20 seconds. Add the onion, cover and braise for 3–5 minutes until golden brown and cooked through, stirring occasionally. Add the Red and Green Masalas and curry leaves, followed by the undrained poppy seeds, salt and turmeric. Stir continuously for 1 minute. Reduce the heat and stir in the water. Cover and simmer for 30 minutes, until more than half of the water has evaporated. The curry should be thick, but not stiff.

3. Add the green pepper and fresh fenugreek. Continue to simmer for about 10 minutes, until the excess water has evaporated and the poppy seeds leave little or no streaks when stirred.

Garnish with Warm Masala and fresh coriander. Serve on its own as a starter with 'Classic Roti' (p. 147).

Hints and variations
Substitute the fresh fenugreek with any green leafy herb or vegetable: shredded spinach, fresh coriander, and so on. If, at the end of step 1, a significant amount of the poppy seeds remains whole, add extra water and steam until these no longer 'pop' when bitten or squeezed. Cook this dish until it is mushy!

Meat and Poultry

Masalas wreathe and adorn meat and poultry
in a host of tastes – every bite is pure,
tender seduction. Cardamom, cloves and
cinnamon move to the fore as the main
supporting flavours.

You'll find the pick of the meat and poultry recipes we know in these pages – a hearty selection that aims, like every chapter in this book, to show how masalas work within a particular category of cuisine. And tempt the little dog-earing devil in you! This chapter debunks 'the Great Marinating Myth,' which holds that meat should stand for hours in its marinade before cooking. In fact, once you've made your paste of masala and spices, you need simply rub it in and start cooking right away. Of course, there's no harm in placing the marinated meat in the fridge for half a day – but we're betting that you won't taste any difference in the result!

Meat is meant to carry many flavours: cardamom pods, cloves and cinnamon sticks, all very strong, are the right-hand spices of the masalas in these dishes. And meat is generally a social food – it pays to make plenty, except on those romantic occasions for two. A highlight for social gatherings is 'Mince Kebabs' on p. 81. Tangy meatballs seared over white-hot coals until sizzling with juices – this one's sure to be dog-eared for the summer!

The universal first step when preparing meat is to trim and wash it (except mince, which is usually pre-washed: never wash mince). Remove excess fat, place the meat or chicken in a bowl, sprinkle it with a few teaspoons of salt, cover it with water and allow it to soak for 2–3 minutes. Drain and you're ready to go. Remember, meat on the bone generally gives best results in curries, though cubed meat will satisfy the billing nicely, too.

Classic Chicken Curry

Preparation time: 15 minutes Cooking time: 45 minutes Serves 4–6
Red Masala, Warm Masala

The chicken curry you've always dreamed of.

1.5 kg skinned chicken pieces
2 tsp salt
2 tsp Red Masala
2 tsp turmeric
1 tsp water or white vinegar
2 Tbsp oil
1 finely chopped onion
2 peeled potatoes, sliced into large pieces
½ peeled gem squash, finely diced
½ cup water
2 finely chopped tomatoes

PAN SPICES
8–10 cinnamon stick pieces
3–4 whole cloves
3–4 cardamom pods

TO GARNISH
½ tsp Warm Masala
2 heaped Tbsp fresh coriander

1. Trim the excess fat from the chicken pieces and cut into medium 'cubes' through the bone joints (leaving the drumsticks whole). Score the pieces deeply.

2. Place the chicken in a medium-sized bowl. Make a paste of the salt, Red Masala, turmeric and 1 tsp of water or white vinegar, and rub thoroughly into the chicken pieces.

3. Heat the oil in a wide pot on medium-high. When hot, add the cinnamon, cloves and cardamom, stir and allow to sizzle for about 30 seconds. Reduce the heat, add the onion and stir well. Cover and braise for 3–5 minutes until golden brown and thoroughly cooked. Stir occasionally.

4. Add the chicken to the pot, stir and cover, cooking for 7–10 minutes, until the chicken begins to yield its juices. Add the potatoes, squash, ¼ cup of water and stir. Cover and simmer for 10 minutes. Add the tomatoes and stir in gently. Add another ¼ cup of water, cover and simmer for a final 10 minutes. The dish is done when the chicken and potatoes are cooked through.

Sprinkle with Warm Masala and coriander. Serve warm with 'Plain Rice' (p. 143).

Hints and variations
The diced squash can be substituted with grated butternut. For additional tang and a darker red colour, add 1 tsp fresh, finely chopped ginger and 1 tsp chilli powder with the chicken in step 4.

See photograph on page 74

Lamb Chops

Preparation time: 15 minutes Cooking time: 55 minutes Serves 4
Red Masala, Warm Masala

This is one of the best 'dry' meat curries. Prepared with succulent cabbage strips, the lamb chops are served glistening, dressed in a rich array of spices. A dish for fine dining at home.

500 g trimmed lamb chops
½ tsp salt
1 tsp Red Masala
1 tsp turmeric
1 tsp water or oil
3 Tbsp oil
½ finely chopped onion
2 peeled potatoes, sliced into large pieces
1¼ cup water
½ finely chopped tomato
⅛ head shredded green cabbage
(about 100g/2 cups)

PAN SPICES
2 cardamom pods
3–4 whole cloves
5–6 cinnamon stick pieces

TO GARNISH
½ tsp Warm Masala
1 heaped Tbsp finely chopped fresh coriander

1. Place the chops in a bowl, sprinkle with ½ tsp salt, cover with water and soak for 2–3 minutes. Drain, rinse, and drain again. Open each chop by slicing from one bone end into the main part of the meat, creating a flap. Score in several places.

2. Make a paste of the salt, Red Masala, turmeric and 1 tsp water or oil, and rub thoroughly into the meat. Heat the oil in a wide pot on medium. When hot, add the cardamom pods, cloves and cinnamon sticks, stir and allow to sizzle for about 30 seconds. Add the onion, cover and braise for 3–5 minutes until golden brown and cooked through. Stir occasionally.

3. Reduce the heat, then add the lamb chops, stirring well. Cover and brown the chops for about 25 minutes, allowing the meat juices to reduce to a thick brown gravy. Turn the chops after 20 minutes.

4. Add the potatoes and stir. Add 1 cup water, cover and simmer for 20 minutes, stirring carefully every 5 minutes. Add water by the quarter cupful if necessary to prevent scorching.

5. Sprinkle the tomato over the lamb, followed by the shredded cabbage. Add ¼ cup water, cover and simmer for 5 minutes, until the tomato melts into the dish and the cabbage wilts.

6. Turn the chops and potatoes. Garnish with Warm Masala and coriander, and continue to cook undisturbed until all the excess water has steamed off. The dish should be very moist, but with little or no gravy.

Serve warm with rice.

Hints and variations
This dish can be prepared in a frying pan without potatoes.

Mince Kebabs

Preparation time: 10 minutes Marinating time: minimum 1 hour up to 12 hours
Cooking time: 15 minutes Serves 4–6 Yields 50
Green Masala, Red Masala, Warm Masala

Interestingly for a meat recipe, Green Masala takes pride of place here, lending its extra-fresh 'bite' to the mince, with the 'heat' of the Red Masala taking up the supporting role. Note that this is one of the few meat recipes that requires marinating time. It can even be made the night before and kept in the fridge.

750 g mince (mutton or beef)
2 tsp salt
3 tsp Green Masala
1½ tsp Red Masala
1 tsp Warm Masala
1 tsp grated ginger root
2 tsp turmeric
4 Tbsp finely chopped fresh coriander
½ semi finely chopped onion

1. Mix the salt, masalas and ginger thoroughly into the mince. Add the turmeric 1 tsp at a time and press through the mince with the back of a spoon, until it has acquired a rich yellow hue. Add the fresh coriander, 'kneading' it through the ball of mince. Reserve for a minimum of 1 hour, up to 12 hours.

2. Light the coals and allow them to reach ash-white hotness (between 20 and 40 minutes). Before forming the kebab balls (about 10 minutes before cooking – the coals should be close to their hottest) mix the onion thoroughly into the mince. Shape small, firm balls 3–4 cm in diameter (about 50). Don't skewer until just before placing them over the coals, lest the mince loosen on the skewers.

3. Prepare a finger bowl of water and 1 Tbsp vinegar. When the coals are ready, skewer the mince balls, placing as many on the skewers as will fit over the coals, and reshaping them firmly on the skewers. Dip your fingers into the finger bowl every so often to prevent sticking.

4. Lay the skewers 10–15 cm above the coals. Cook the meat for about 15 minutes until well-browned on all sides, turning regularly.

To complete the feast, serve immediately with 'Quick Coriander Chutney' (p. 24), 'Thick Tomato Chutney' (p. 26) and 'Foulka' (p. 156) or rolls.

Hints and variations

When choosing mince, try to find some that is dry and stiff (but still fresh) rather than moist and mushy. If you cook the kebabs when the fire is too cool, the individual balls may drop off the skewers, because the water from the onions will cause them to loosen and lose shape. Similarly, if you add onions to the mince at the outset (at marinating stage), they will give off water and ruin the mince. If dry, stiff mince is not available, omit the onion altogether. The balls can also be fried in a wide frying pan instead of roasted over coals.

Crumbed Chicken

Preparation time: 5 minutes (skinned chicken) 15 minutes (unskinned chicken)
Cooking time: 45 minutes Serves 4
Red Masala, Warm Masala

This is the tastiest and healthiest fried chicken we know. The chicken pieces are prepared skinless, and simmered until done before pan frying, so the amount of oil required is nominal.

1.5 kg skinned chicken drumsticks and thighs
1½ tsp salt
1½ tsp Red Masala
1 tsp turmeric
1 tsp Warm Masala
½ tsp chilli powder
½ Tbsp oil (marinade)
2 tsp lemon juice
4 Tbsp oil
2 large eggs
½ cup fresh or dried breadcrumbs

PAN SPICES
2 cardamom pods
3–4 whole cloves
4–5 cinnamon stick pieces

TO GARNISH
1 heaped Tbsp finely chopped fresh coriander

1. Trim the chicken pieces of excess fat, rinse and drain. Dry on kitchen paper. Score, cutting deeply into the dark and pink flesh.

2. Prepare the marinade. Mix 1 tsp salt, the Red Masala, turmeric, Warm Masala, chilli powder, oil and lemon juice into a thick paste. Rub well into the chicken and reserve for 5 minutes.

3. Heat 2 Tbsp oil in a wide, deep pot on medium. When hot, add the cardamom, cloves and cinnamon, stir and allow to sizzle for about 30 seconds. Add the chicken pieces, stir, cover, and allow to simmer in their own juices for 30–35 minutes, until the juices have cooked away. Stir occasionally to prevent sticking. Note that some light scorching is inevitable. Remove from the pot, and drain on kitchen paper.

4. While the chicken is cooking, beat the eggs, mixing in ½ tsp salt. Pour the breadcrumbs into a wide, shallow bowl.

5. Heat 2 Tbsp oil in a wide, non-stick pan on high. Dip 3–4 chicken pieces in the egg and roll in the breadcrumbs until well coated. Immediately place the pieces in the pan. Fry 1 minute per side, turning twice, for a total cooking time of about 3 minutes per piece. Remove as soon as the chicken browns slightly.

Drain on kitchen paper. Garnish with fresh coriander. Serve with 'Plain Rice' (p. 143) or 'Quick Coriander Chutney' (p. 24).

Mince Curry

Preparation time: 5 minutes Cooking time: 50 minutes Serves 4
Red Masala, Warm Masala

This recipe is so easy to prepare – even by masala standards – that it almost feels like cheating. Mince is no-hassle food: there's no worrying about whether the meat is cooked through or tender enough, and complementary ingredients can be added and subtracted as you please. Fortunately, there's also no direct link between the amount of time spent at the stove and the scrumptiousness of the result!

1½ tsp salt
1½ tsp Red Masala
2 tsp turmeric
1 tsp finely chopped ginger root
2 tsp vinegar
400 g mince
2½ Tbsp oil
1 finely chopped onion
2 peeled potatoes, sliced into medium pieces
1½ cups water
100 g fresh or frozen peas (about 1 cup)
2 grated tomatoes

PAN SPICES
2–3 cardamom pods
3–4 whole cloves
4–5 cinnamon stick pieces

TO GARNISH
1 tsp Warm Masala
2 heaped Tbsp finely chopped fresh coriander

1. Prepare the marinade. Mix the salt, Red Masala, turmeric, ginger and vinegar into a paste. Press this through the mince thoroughly with the back of a spoon.

2. Heat 2 Tbsp oil in a deep, wide pot on medium-high. When hot, add the cardamom, cloves and cinnamon, stir and allow to sizzle for about 30 seconds. Add the onion, cover and braise for 3–5 minutes until golden brown and cooked through, stirring occasionally.

3. Add the mince to the pot and mix it well with the onion. Cover and brown for 10–12 minutes, until the mince juices have burned away. (Note that browning time depends on the leanness of the mince.) Stir regularly, breaking up the mince to prevent clumping.

4. Reduce the heat, add the potatoes and stir once. Cover, cook for 5 minutes, then add ½ Tbsp oil and ¼ cup water. Cover and simmer for 10 minutes.

5. Mix the peas and grated tomatoes in a bowl, then spoon over the mince. Add 1¼ cup water, stir once gently, cover and simmer for 15 minutes. The dish is done when the potatoes are cooked through. Adjust for the desired amount of gravy by adding water in small amounts.

Garnish with Warm Masala and fresh coriander, and serve with 'Classic Roti' (p. 147).

Chicken Meatballs

Preparation time: 30 minutes Cooking time: 20 minutes Serves 4–6 Yields 30
Red Masala, Warm Masala

This is one of our favourites – a gourmet feast. The Red and Warm Masalas are drafted into double duty, making an especially rich sauce for the excellent meatballs. The dish is surprisingly quick to put together.

2 peeled potatoes, sliced into medium pieces
1 cup water
400 g chicken mince
3½ Tbsp oil
1 finely chopped onion, in ¼ and ¾ portions
2 heaped Tbsp finely chopped fresh coriander
2 grated tomatoes

MEATBALL SPICES
½ tsp salt
1 tsp Red Masala
1½ tsp turmeric
¾ tsp Warm Masala

GRAVY SPICES
¼ tsp salt
¼ tsp Red Masala
¼ tsp turmeric

PAN SPICES
2–3 cardamom pods
2–3 whole cloves
4–5 cinnamon stick pieces

TO GARNISH
½ tsp Warm Masala
1 Tbsp finely chopped fresh coriander

1. Parboil the potatoes. Simmer ½ cup water in a small pot, reduce the heat and add the potatoes. Cover and simmer for 15 minutes.

2. Prepare the chicken meatballs. Press the meatball spices thoroughly into the mince, followed by 1½ Tbsp oil, the ¼ onion portion and the fresh coriander. Prepare a finger bowl of water. Shape the mince into about 30 small egg-shaped balls, each about 4 cm long. Dip your fingers in the finger bowl to prevent sticking.

3. Heat 2 Tbsp oil in a wide pot on medium-high. When hot, add the cardamom, cloves and cinnamon (pan spices), stir, and allow to sizzle for about 30 seconds. Add the ¾ onion portion, stir once, then add the salt, Red Masala and turmeric (gravy spices). Stir well, cover and braise for 3–5 minutes, until the onion is cooked through.

4. Reduce the heat, then place the chicken meatballs into the onion mixture one by one, until the base of the pot is covered. This is the first layer. Add 2 Tbsp water to the pot to prevent sticking, cover and steam for 3 minutes.

5. Turn the meatballs (some will have browned). Add the remaining meatballs to the top of the first layer. Add an additional 2 Tbsp water, cover and steam for 2–3 minutes.

6. Add the parboiled potatoes. Spoon the grated tomatoes over the meatballs and potatoes, add ¼ cup water, stir gently, and simmer for 5 minutes.

Sprinkle with Warm Masala and fresh coriander. Serve with 'Classic Roti' (p. 147) or 'Plain Rice' (p. 143).

Hints and variations

For more gravy when serving with rice, add an extra ¼ cup water with the tomatoes in step 6, and salt to taste. Don't substitute chicken mince with other kinds of mince, because of the way the different meats interact with onions.

Roast Leg of Lamb

Preparation time: 15 minutes Marinating time: 6–12 hours Cooking time: 1½ hours Serves 4–6
Red Masala, Warm Masala, Three-spice Masala

Ask your butcher for a cut from the middle part of the lower leg, between the knee and lower shin, and request that the cut be skinned and trimmed of fat.

1 kg leg of lamb
salt for rubbing
1½ tsp coriander seeds
½ tsp salt
1½ tsp Red Masala
1 heaped tsp Three-spice Masala
1 heaped tsp Warm Masala
½ tsp turmeric
1 tsp chilli powder
2 tsp grated ginger
4 Tbsp oil
2 cups water
4 peeled and quartered potatoes

PAN SPICES
6–8 cinnamon stick pieces
3–4 whole cloves
2–3 whole cardamom pods

TO GARNISH
3 Tbsp finely chopped fresh coriander

1. Prepare the leg of lamb. Remove any excess fat, as well as the vein beneath the leg bone, if necessary. Rub any red parts with salt. Wash the leg thoroughly in a bowl under a tap and drain. Pat dry with kitchen paper, and score deeply in several places.

2. Marinate the leg. Coarsely crush the coriander seeds in a mortar, then mix with the salt, Red, Three-spice and Warm Masalas, turmeric, chilli powder and ginger. Add 1 Tbsp oil and mix the ingredients into a thick paste. Rub it well into the leg and scorings.

3. Heat 3 Tbsp oil in a deep, wide pot on medium. When hot, add the pan spices, stir and allow to sizzle for about 30 seconds. Place the leg in the pot carefully, and cover. Turn three times at 5-minute intervals, until the entire leg is browned, yielding juices on all sides.

4. Reduce the heat, add 2 cups of water, and cover. Simmer for 45 minutes. Add water by the ¼ cupful to prevent scorching.

5. Surround the roast with the potatoes, cover and cook for 20 minutes until done, adding water if necessary. Sprinkle with 2 Tbsp coriander, cover and cook for a final 3–5 minutes.

Remove the roast and potatoes for serving, and garnish with the remaining 1 Tbsp coriander. Serve slices of roast with a vegetable side dish (for instance, 'Spicy Cauli-flower', p. 50). Collect the juices and scrapings from the pot to spread over the roast slices.

Ghosht Dhal

Preparation time: 15 minutes Soaking time: 30 minutes Cooking time: 1 hour 45 minutes Serves 4
Red Masala, Warm Masala

Ghosht Dhal is Indian cuisine's own chicken soup. A piping hot bowl is sure fortification against the energy consuming challenges of modern living. 'Ghosht' refers to the lamb bones that are simmered with the delicious, warming oil dhal. There's just one rule to follow when preparing this dish: cook and cook and cook! Just keep adding water and keep it simmering along.

1¼ cups oil (toovar) dhal
water for soaking
2 tsp salt
½ tsp Red Masala
1 tsp turmeric
½ tsp grated ginger root
250 g lamb rib bones, lean of meat
1½ Tbsp oil
½ finely chopped onion
2½ cups water, at room temperature
¼ tsp fenugreek seeds
3½ cups freshly boiled water
2 finely chopped tomatoes
1 Tbsp lemon juice

PAN SPICES
3–4 cinnamon stick pieces
3–4 whole cloves

TO GARNISH
½ tsp Warm Masala
2 Tbsp finely chopped fresh coriander

1. Rinse the dhal under a tap, drain in a colander, then soak in lukewarm water for 30 minutes. (For convenience, soak while the meat bones are simmering, steps 2–3.)

2. Make a paste of the salt, Red Masala, turmeric and ginger. Rub it well into the lamb bones. Heat the oil in a large pot on medium-high. When hot, add the cinnamon and cloves, stir and allow to sizzle for about 30 seconds. Add the onion, cover and braise for 3–5 minutes until golden brown and cooked through, stirring occasionally. Add the ribs, and braise in the onion for 7–10 minutes, stirring well.

3. Reduce the heat. Add 1 cup of water at room temperature, cover and simmer for 50 minutes until the meat is very tender and the juices have reduced to a thick gravy. Add water by the quarter cupful if necessary.

4. Drain the dhal, add it to the ribs and stir once. Raise the heat and add the fenugreek seeds and freshly boiled water. Bring the pot to a simmer, then reduce the heat, partially cover and simmer slowly for 30 minutes. (Guard against boiling over.) The dhal will become thick and soupy, and the dhal grains will soften and break up.

5. Add the tomatoes, lemon juice and 1½ cups water, cover partially and continue to simmer for 15–20 minutes, until the desired gravy thickness is reached.

Garnish with Warm Masala and coriander. Serve over rice or on its own in soup bowls. 'Carrot Atchar' (p. 33) is a good accompaniment.

Hints and variations

If rib bones aren't available, any small lamb bones that are lean of meat will do. This dhal thickens when it stands overnight: to reheat, add ¼–½ cup water and a pinch of salt. For a delicious, rich variation, garnish each bowl served with a dollop of cream or a blob of ghee. For a different consistency, add a few shredded spinach leaves with the tomato in step 5.

Lamb Curry

Preparation time: 10 minutes Cooking time: 1 hour Serves 4
Red Masala, Warm Masala

A classic curry. If there is an Indian approximation of 'meat and potatoes', this is it! We prefer to cook on-the-bone lamb because of the extra juices and flavours it yields, which in turn ensure perfectly tender meat. Plain lamb steak does nicely, too – just simmer it a bit longer.

500 g lamb pieces, on-the-bone, or
400 g cubed lamb steak
1 tsp salt
1½ tsp Red Masala
1½ tsp turmeric
2½ Tbsp oil
1 finely chopped onion
2 peeled potatoes, sliced into large pieces
¼ cup water
100 g halved and thinly sliced green beans
1 finely chopped tomato

PAN SPICES
3–4 whole cloves
4–5 cinnamon stick pieces
2–3 cardamom pods

TO GARNISH
1 tsp Warm Masala
2 Tbsp finely chopped fresh coriander

1. Trim the lamb pieces of excess fat and score well. Mix the salt, Red Masala and turmeric into a dry paste, and rub into the lamb until all the pieces are well-covered. One tsp of oil may be added to help stretch the marinade.

2. Heat the oil in a deep pot on medium-high. When hot, add the pan spices, stir and allow to sizzle for 30 seconds. Add the onion, cover and braise for 3–5 minutes until golden brown and cooked through. Stir occasionally.

3. Reduce the heat and add the lamb to the pot, stirring once. Cover and brown for about 25 minutes, stirring occasionally, until most of the juices have cooked away.

4. Add the potatoes and ¼ cup water. Cover and simmer for 10 minutes, stirring occasionally.

5. Sprinkle the beans over the lamb and potatoes, but do not stir. Cover and simmer for 10 minutes. Add water by the quarter cupful if necessary to prevent scorching.

6. Add the tomato, spooning it over the dish rather than stirring it in. Cover and continue to simmer for a final 10 minutes.

Garnish with Warm Masala and fresh coriander, and serve with 'Plain Rice' (p. 143) and 'Quick Coriander Chutney' (p. 24).

Hints and variations
Always choose lamb from the loin for this recipe, not the rib or other parts (the loin is the most tender cut) and be sure to select fresh, crisp green beans to accompany the meat.

Seafood Dishes

A sprinkling or spackling of masala transforms your fish, crustaceans or prawns into indescribably delectable morsels. Curry leaves and fenugreek seeds play complementary roles.

This is quite possibly our favourite chapter. The reason? It's a toss-up between 'Fried Snoek' on p. 98, 'Crayfish Curry' on p. 100, and 'Prawn Curry' on p. 110. OK – Crayfish Curry wins, hands-down, actually! These can't-go-wrong curries place seafood paradise within easy reach.

We'll save further raptures for the recipe itself. The principal gist of 'Crayfish Curry' and its companions over the next several pages is this: masala and seafood were made for each other. With these can't-go-wrong curries, seafood paradise is within reach.

Remember that all fish or shellfish must be fresh-fresh. (Say that five times fast!) Fish should never smell fishy: if it does, you know it's been standing a bit long. There are times, however, when it's impossible to find 100% fresh fish, in which case it must be washed with extra care. Basic washing instructions: place the fish in a wide bowl of cold water, sprinkle it with 4 tsp salt, add a Tbsp of white vinegar, and soak for 5 minutes. (Never put fish directly under the tap.) Drain carefully and dry on kitchen paper. As with meat and poultry, most seafood recipes call for little or no marinating time, meaning you can prepare them in a trice. When you're stuck for something delectable, and don't want too much fuss, think fish!

Gravy Fish

Preparation time: 20 minutes Cooking time: 30 minutes Serves 4
Red Masala, Three-spice Masala, Warm Masala

Follow this recipe for fish that simmers to perfect doneness in a beautiful red-orange gravy, and slips off the fork in delightfully succulent bites.

500 g hake medallions or similar fish
(5–7 slices, on the bone)
2 tsp salt
2 tsp Red Masala
1 tsp turmeric
1 Tbsp vinegar
2 Tbsp oil
¼ finely chopped onion
5 finely chopped very ripe tomatoes
8–9 torn or lightly crushed curry leaves
(fresh or dried)
1 Tbsp lemon juice
1½ tsp Three-spice Masala
½ cup water

PAN SPICE
½ tsp fenugreek seeds

TO GARNISH
½ tsp Warm Masala
2 heaped Tbsp finely chopped fresh coriander

1. Taking care not to over-handle the medallions, pick out any veins around the spine with the tip of a knife, and remove any tissue. (See opposite page for instructions on how to wash the fish.)

2. Mix the salt, Red Masala, turmeric and vinegar into a paste. Rub this gently into both sides of each fish medallion. Set aside.

3. Heat the oil in a wide pot on medium. When hot, add the fenugreek seeds and stir once. Add the onion, cover and braise for 3–5 minutes until golden brown and cooked through. Stir occasionally. Add the tomatoes, cover and cook for a further 6–8 minutes, until well amalgamated with the onion.

4. Reduce the heat, add the curry leaves and stir. Place the fish medallions gently into the tomato gravy, allowing them to set into place. Neither flip the fish nor stir the pot during the rest of the cooking – just tilt the pot gently from side to side to mix the ingredients. Add the lemon juice and cover, allowing the fish to steam for 8–10 minutes.

5. Sprinkle Three-spice Masala over the fish, add the water and spoon the gravy over the fish. Simmer, covered, for a final 2–3 minutes.

Garnish with Warm Masala and coriander. Serve the medallions on a bed of 'Plain Rice' (p. 143) with a few spoonfuls of gravy.

Hints and variations
When ordering medallions, have the fins and scales removed, and the fish sliced on-the-bone from the head end toward the tail. Each piece should be 1.5–2 cm thick, and not more than 15 cm in diameter. To thicken the gravy, add a paste of 1 tsp chickpea (gram) dhal flour, ½ Tbsp cake (plain) flour, and 1½ Tbsp gravy during step 4.

Fried Snoek

Preparation time: 10–20 minutes (depending on fish preparation – see note)
Marinating time: 30 minutes Cooking time: 25 minutes Serves 4
Red Masala, Three-spice Masala, Warm Masala

This is one of our favourites. We call it a 'just because' recipe: you make it just because the fish is available, not necessarily because lunch, dinner or guests have motivated you to cook. One taste of these fiery, lip-smacking morsels, and you'll plan your week around the next batch. Unlike the preceding recipe, not every kind of fish will do here: it must be dense, meaty and thick – able to hold together during intense frying.

FISH PREPARATION

Fish to order: ask for a piece from the middle part of the fish, nearest the head. Have the fins and scales removed, the fish opened and cleaned, and cut in half lengthwise along the spine, so that the spine is flush to one side of its half. Have these two pieces quartered for a total of 8 pieces. Soak them in cold water for 5 minutes, sprinkled with 2–3 tsp salt. Drain and dry on kitchen paper.

Whole fish: have the head, tail, fins and any scales removed, the fish opened and cleaned, and cut widthwise across the spine into wide strips. Fill a tub with cold water and add 5 tsp salt. Soak the strips for 5 minutes. Drain and dry on kitchen paper. Lay the strips skin side down, then cut lengthwise (along the spine) into four strips. Cut these strips in half widthwise into square pieces. Select 6–8 pieces for frying. Dry them on kitchen paper. Wrap the remaining pieces into small packages for keeping in the deep freeze.

Note: if the fish smells at all 'fishy,' add 2 Tbsp white vinegar when soaking.

2 tsp salt
2½ tsp Red Masala
4 tsp Warm Masala
1 tsp Three-spice Masala
1 tsp turmeric
2 Tbsp white vinegar
700 g snoek or similar fish
6 Tbsp oil

PAN SPICE
½ tsp fenugreek seeds

TO GARNISH
1 heaped Tbsp finely chopped fresh coriander (optional)

1. Mix the salt, Red, Warm and Three-spice Masalas and turmeric into a dry paste. Add the vinegar and mix in well, then rub the paste into all sides of the fish pieces, until evenly coated and dark orange in colour. Flecks of Red Masala should be visible on the fish. Reserve in a bowl for up to 30 minutes.

2. Heat the oil in a large, non-stick frying pan on high. When hot, add the fenugreek seeds, stir once and allow to sizzle for about 10 seconds. Place the fish pieces skin side down in the pan and cover with a splatter screen. Fry for 2 minutes.

3. Reduce the heat and continue frying. Turn the pieces with a spatula or fork after 5 minutes. The skin side should be well browned. Cover with the splatter screen and fry for a further 3–4 minutes, adding an additional Tbsp oil if needed. Turn again, fry on the skin side for a final 3 minutes until the fish is thoroughly cooked.

4. Remove the pan from the heat. Allow the fish to cool in the pan.

Sprinkle the snoek with fresh coriander (optional). Serve hot, on its own, or with 'Plain Rice' (p. 143).

Hints and variations

If snoek is unavailable in your area, any firm, white-fleshed fish makes a good substitute. Don't forget that each piece of fish should have skin on one side.

If you don't have an extractor fan above your stove, ensure your kitchen is well-ventilated before you start. And in all situations keep the splatter screen handy!

Crayfish Curry

Preparation time: 30 minutes Cooking time: 25 minutes Serves 2
Red Masala, Three-spice Masala, Warm Masala

This is a sensational dish, one of our favourites. There is no finer marriage of the fruits of the sea with the flavours of Indian cuisine. The large, lobster-like crayfish, native to South Africa's coast, used to be the most commonly available seafood at the harbourside, a factor which no doubt contributed to the dish's exquisite simplicity. The main effort here lies in properly dividing the crayfish into smaller pieces. For this spectacular curry's best-kept secret, see the hint following the recipe.

CRAYFISH PREPARATION

Defrost, if frozen, in a bowl of water at room temperature, then lay out on kitchen paper to dry. Cut the tail from the main body at the joint, remove the tail fan and the underside tail fins. Slice into the underside tail flesh lengthwise (merely cut into the flesh: do not cut the tail in half), locate the central vein and food bag (a long, clear, liquid-filled lining) with the tip of a knife, and remove, along with any sand in the area around the food bag. Cut the tail into thirds widthwise. Sprinkle 2 tsp salt into a wide bowl filled with water, and soak the tail pieces in the bowl.

Remove the central body legs, and the spurs and nails from each leg. Place the legs in the bowl with the tail pieces. Remove the head just behind the eye, cutting from the side, not the top, and discard. Remove the two large, spiny forelegs, and pound gently with a mallet to crack the shell slightly. Place in the bowl. Open the body by placing your thumbs against the top and bottom shells of the central carapace and pulling it apart. Remove the central organs and grey, hairy flesh of the sides. Cut the lower body in half lengthwise (or into quarters if very large), place in the bowl, and soak for 5 minutes. Drain the crayfish in a colander and rinse gently.

2 whole fresh or frozen crayfish, or
700 g–1 kg crayfish pieces
(especially the tail), in the shell
1½ tsp salt
¾ tsp Red Masala
¾ tsp turmeric
1 tsp vinegar
1½ Tbsp oil
¼ finely chopped onion
3 finely chopped tomatoes
6–7 torn or lightly crushed curry leaves
(fresh or dried)
1 heaped tsp chickpea (gram) dhal flour
1½ Tbsp water
½ cup water
½ tsp Three-spice Masala
1½ heaped Tbsp finely chopped
fresh coriander

PAN SPICE
¼ tsp fenugreek seeds

TO GARNISH
½ tsp Warm Masala
2 heaped Tbsp finely chopped fresh coriander

1. Make a paste of the salt, Red Masala, turmeric and vinegar. Turn the crayfish pieces through the spices in a wide bowl, until well-coated. Set aside.

2. Heat the oil in a large pot on medium-high. When hot, add the fenugreek seeds, stir and allow to sizzle for about 10 seconds. Add the onion, cover and braise for 3–5 minutes until golden brown and cooked through. Stir occasionally.

3. Reduce the heat. Add the tomatoes and curry leaves and stir. Simmer, uncovered, for 5–7 minutes until the onions and tomatoes are well amalgamated.

4. Reduce the heat to medium-low. Add the crayfish, stir in gently, and cover. Simmer for 6–10 minutes, until the crayfish has yielded most of its juices. Make a thin paste of the flour and 1½ Tbsp water in a small bowl, stirring until smooth. Add the paste to the curry with ½ cup water.

Stir in the Three-spice Masala and fresh coriander. Reduce the heat to low, cover and simmer for an additional 5 minutes.

Garnish with Warm Masala and coriander. Serve warm over 'Plain Rice' (p. 143), or see the hint below for a scrumptious twist.

Hints and variations
Here is the secret to increasing the divineness of this dish: don't serve it with rice, but with toasted bread instead. Dip the toast into the gravy, suck the gravy out of the toast, and load up a second slice with crayfish pieces. The gastronomic pleasure is intense! This recipe may be prepared with lobster instead of crayfish. Note that if the crayfish smells at all 'fishy', add 1 Tbsp white vinegar to the bowl together with the salt in step 1.

Fried Hake

Preparation time: 20 minutes Cooking time: 25 minutes Serves 4
Red Masala, Three-spice Masala, Warm Masala

This is our best direct route to steaming hot, crisp-but-moist, melt-in-the-mouth fish that transports the tongue with its sumptuous seasonings. As the recipe calls for hake, you'll know that it's particularly suited to lighter, flakier fish. But your favourite fish – if it isn't hake – is likely to do well, too: just bear in mind that the frying will firm it, so you'll want to avoid anything that's too meaty, like shark.

500 g hake medallions or similar fish, on the bone
¾ tsp salt
1½ tsp Red Masala
½ tsp turmeric
1 tsp Warm Masala
½ tsp Three-spice Masala
2 tsp vinegar or lemon juice
cake flour for sprinkling
3 Tbsp oil

PAN SPICE
½ tsp fenugreek seeds

TO GARNISH
1 Tbsp finely chopped fresh coriander

1. Wash the fish medallions (see instructions, p. 96). Dry both sides on kitchen paper. Carefully remove the central bone from the larger medallions, slicing these in half.

2. Mix the salt, Red Masala, turmeric, Warm Masala and Three-spice Masala into a dry paste. Add the vinegar or lemon juice and mix in well. Rub the paste gently into the medallions (both sides) and reserve for 10–15 minutes.

3. Lightly sprinkle cake flour on the medallions' upper side. Heat the oil in a medium, non-stick pan on high. When hot, add the fenugreek seeds, stir, and allow to sizzle for about 10 seconds. Place the fish medallions flour side down in the pan, cover with a splatter screen, and fry for 4–5 minutes.

4. Sprinkle the upper side of the frying fish lightly with cake flour, but do not flip. Cover with the screen and continue frying for 3 minutes.

5. Reduce the heat. Flip the fish carefully with a spatula. The reverse side should be a bright golden brown. Cover the pan with the splatter screen and fry the second side for 6–8 minutes.

6. Break off a small piece of fish to test: it should be cooked through and firm. If not, add ½ Tbsp oil to the pan and continue frying for a final 3–4 minutes.

Remove the pan from the heat. Sprinkle with fresh coriander. Serve immediately with steaming 'Plain Rice' (p. 143).

Hints and variations
Fish as prepared in this recipe doesn't scorch too quickly: make sure to fry it long enough so that it is very firm, longer than called for if necessary. If the fish begins to blacken or burn at any time before it is quite firm, add oil by the ½ tablespoonful.

Fried Crayfish

Preparation time: 15 minutes Cooking time: 30 minutes Serves 2 (starter portion)
Red Masala, Three-spice Masala, Warm Masala

The perfect way to start a romantic dinner for two. Warm Masala's complex flavour carries through particularly well here.

1 whole crayfish, 400–750 g, or 300–500 g
crayfish pieces (especially the tail), in the shell
½ tsp salt
½ tsp Red Masala
½ tsp Three-spice Masala
½ tsp Warm Masala
½ tsp turmeric
1 tsp vinegar
3 Tbsp oil
½ finely chopped onion

PAN SPICE
¼ tsp fenugreek seeds

TO GARNISH
1 heaped Tbsp finely chopped fresh coriander
fresh curry leaves

1. Clean and cut the crayfish as per 'Crayfish Curry' p. 100.

2. Make a paste of the salt, Red, Three-spice and Warm Masalas, turmeric and vinegar. Turn the crayfish pieces through the spices in a wide bowl, until well coated.

3. Heat 2 Tbsp oil in a medium-sized non-stick frying pan on medium-high. When hot, add the fenugreek seeds, stir and allow to sizzle for about 10 seconds. Reduce the heat. Add the crayfish pieces, stir, cover and fry for about 15 minutes, until well-browned on all sides. The crayfish will yield its own juices, which will begin to burn away.

4. Add the remaining Tbsp oil, followed by the onion. Stir, cover and fry for about 5 minutes, until the onions are golden brown and thoroughly cooked. Remove the cover and fry until the remaining crayfish juices have burned away.

Remove the crayfish from the pan and sprinkle with coriander and curry leaves. Serve hot as a starter.

Prawn Biryani

Preparation time: 30 minutes Cooking time: 1 hour Serves 4–6
Red Masala, Green Masala, Warm Masala, Three-spice Masala

This is a four-masala masterpiece, requiring steady effort and attention. Biryani is royal food, comprising a broad medley of tastes, and meant to be rich. Your work of art will be rewarded with royal praise!

200 g medium-sized fresh or frozen prawn tails

2 cups basmati rice (uncooked volume)

½ cup brown lentils

2 peeled potatoes, sliced into medium-sized pieces

4½ Tbsp oil

2 finely chopped cloves garlic

2 Tbsp water for steaming

½ tsp Warm Masala

250 g thinly sliced button mushrooms

¾ cup fresh or frozen peas

10–12 torn or lightly crushed curry leaves (fresh or dried)

7–10 strands saffron

3 Tbsp ghee

½ thickly sliced onion

2 fresh, coarsely chopped green chillies (optional)

4 heaped Tbsp finely chopped fresh coriander

1 tsp chilli powder (optional)

½ tsp Green Masala

PRAWN MARINADE

1 tsp Red Masala

1 tsp salt

½ tsp turmeric

1 tsp vinegar

RICE SPICES

1½ tsp salt

6–7 cinnamon stick pieces

3 cardamom pods

3 whole cloves

pinch turmeric

PAN SPICE (1)

¼ tsp fenugreek seeds

PAN SPICES (2)

½ tsp cumin seeds

½ tsp salt

¼ tsp Red Masala

¼ tsp turmeric

½ tsp Three-spice Masala

1. Clean and rinse the prawns as per 'Prawn Curry', p. 110. Rice: prepare as per 'Plain Rice', p. 143, adding the rice spices indicated here before the pot begins to boil. Lentils: bring to the boil with ½ tsp salt in 2 cups of water, reduce the heat, simmer until soft (about 20 minutes), then drain. Potatoes: bring ½ cup water to a simmer in a small pot, reduce the heat, add the potatoes and cover. Simmer for 15–20 minutes until soft, then drain.

2. Make a paste of the Red Masala, salt, turmeric and vinegar and stir through the prawns in a medium bowl until they are thoroughly coated. Heat 1½ Tbsp oil in a medium-sized frying pan on medium-high. When hot, add one finely chopped garlic clove and the pan spice (1). Stir and allow to sizzle for about 30 seconds. Reduce the heat. Add the prawns, stir, and sauté for 5 minutes, stirring frequently. Reduce the heat again. Add 2 Tbsp water, stir and then add the Warm Masala. Cover and steam for 6–8 minutes, until the prawns are cooked. Remove from

the heat and reserve in a covered dish. Reserve the pan with the prawn juices for step 4.

3. Heat 2 Tbsp oil in a second, large frying pan on medium-high. When hot, add the cumin seeds, stir, and allow to sizzle for about 30 seconds. Add the pan spices (2). Stir once. Add the mushrooms and stir well, exposing them all to the heat of the pan. Sauté, uncovered, for about 8 minutes, until most of the mushroom juices have burned away. Reduce the heat, add the peas and curry leaves, stir and cover. Simmer for 3–5 minutes, until all the excess water has burned away. Remove from the heat.

4. Place the saffron strands in a small bowl filled with 3–4 Tbsp hot water, and leave to soak. Heat 1 Tbsp oil and 1 Tbsp ghee on medium in the prawn pan. When hot, add the second garlic clove and onion slices and sauté for 6–8 minutes, until the onion is a dark golden brown and slightly crispy, with 'burnt' or 'scorched' tips. Remove from the heat.

5. Heat 1½ Tbsp ghee in a large, deep pot. Add the fresh green chillies. Cover the base of the pot with two layers of a third of the rice and lentils, half of the potatoes, half of the mushrooms and peas, half of the prawns, and a third of the onions. Sprinkle each layer with 1 Tbsp of the saffron water, ½ tsp chilli powder, and 1 Tbsp fresh coriander. Fold the two layers of biryani into each other with a large spoon. Add the Green Masala, and cover with the remaining rice and lentils. Add the remaining third onion, and drizzle with the rest of the saffron water. Add 2 Tbsp coriander and ½ Tbsp ghee, and allow to melt into the rice. Gently fold the layers into each other again. Cover and steam for 10 minutes (ensure the heat is on low to avoid scorching), stirring gently every 3–4 minutes.

Serve warm with 'Green Masala Buttermilk' (p. 27).

Hints and variations
For a slightly sweeter, richer flavour, add ½ grated onion with the first layer of rice in step 5.

Sardine Sarmie

Cooking time: 20 minutes Serves 2
Red Masala, Three-spice Masala, Warm Masala

*The transforming powers of masala are on full display here. Ordinary, rather plain sardines become a flavoursome feast.
This is fantastic food for the road, cooked up in a trice.*

240 g (2 tins) sardines
1½ Tbsp oil
1 finely chopped onion
½ tsp salt
¼ tsp Red Masala
¼ tsp turmeric
¼ tsp Three-spice Masala
6–7 torn or lightly crushed curry leaves
(fresh or dried)
1 finely chopped tomato
¼ tsp Warm Masala
1 Tbsp water
1 heaped Tbsp finely chopped fresh coriander
fresh bread or rolls

PAN SPICE
¼ tsp fenugreek seeds

TO GARNISH
1 heaped Tbsp finely chopped fresh coriander

1. Drain sardine tins of any oil or brine.

2. Heat the oil in a medium-sized, non-stick frying pan on medium. When hot, add the fenugreek seeds, stir and allow to sizzle for about 20 seconds. Add the onion, cover and braise for 3–5 minutes until golden brown and cooked through. Stir occasionally.

3. Add the salt, Red Masala, turmeric, Three-spice Masala and curry leaves. Stir well. Add the tomato, stir, cover and cook for about 5 minutes, until well amalgamated with the onion.

4. Lay the sardines in the tomato-and-onion mixture and break up with a fork. Add the Warm Masala, water and fresh coriander, and stir. Spoon the curry over the fish, cover and simmer for 5–7 minutes, turning once.

Garnish with fresh coriander. Serve warm or cold on fresh bread, rolls or ciabatta with other sandwich ingredients such as cheese, sliced tomato, and fresh basil leaves.

Hints and variations
The coriander may be replaced with fresh fenugreek.

Prawn Curry

Preparation time: 20 minutes Cooking time 20 minutes Serves 4
Red Masala, Three-spice Masala, Warm Masala

We recommend adopting this recipe as an automatic first choice for satisfying a seafood craving, particularly when you're in no mood for even modest culinary acrobatics. You may want to memorise it! Prawns are pure convenience, requiring no preparation aside from de-veining (and you can even skip that simple step, though don't tell anyone we said so), and they simmer to perfection in under half an hour.

PRAWN PREPARATION

If frozen, soak the prawns in water for about 5 minutes, until they begin to separate. Drain, splash with 1 Tbsp white vinegar, soak in fresh water for 2–3 minutes, then drain again. If the prawns aren't frozen, or aren't clean (i.e. are sandy, or have parts that are turning brown or black), soak for 5 minutes in water with 1 tsp salt and 1 Tbsp vinegar. Drain and splash with 1 Tbsp vinegar. Soak in clean water for a further 1–2 minutes and drain. Remove any black or brown spots with a sharp knife.

De-vein the prawns by slicing open part of the top shell, locating the central vein with the tip of a knife and drawing it out gently. If the vein breaks, slice open the entire top part of the shell, and pull out the vein pieces. Leaving the prawn in the shell, remove the head and legs. Don't remove the entire shell.

200 g medium fresh or frozen prawns
1 tsp salt
½ tsp Red Masala
¾ tsp turmeric
1½ Tbsp oil
¼ finely chopped onion
7–8 torn or lightly crushed curry leaves (fresh or dried)
4 grated very ripe tomatoes
½ tsp Three-spice Masala
1½ Tbsp finely chopped fresh coriander
½ cup water
½ tsp tomato paste (optional)

PAN SPICE
½ tsp fenugreek seeds

TO GARNISH
¼ tsp Warm Masala
1 Tbsp finely chopped fresh coriander

1. Place the prawns in a bowl. Add the salt, Red Masala and turmeric, and turn the prawns gently through the spices with a spoon. Reserve.

2. Heat the oil in a medium-sized pot on medium-high. When hot, add the fenugreek seeds, stir, and allow to sizzle for about 10 seconds. Add the onion and curry leaves and stir well. Cover and braise for 3–5 minutes until the onion is golden brown and cooked through, stirring occasionally.

3. Reduce the heat, add the tomatoes and stir thoroughly. Simmer, covered, for 5 minutes, until the tomatoes are well amalgamated with the onion.

4. Reduce the heat again. Add the prawns, Three-spice Masala and fresh coriander. Stir. Add the water and tomato paste, cover and simmer for 5–7 minutes, until the prawns are cooked through.

Garnish with Warm Masala and fresh coriander. Serve hot with 'Plain Rice' (p. 143).

Hints and variations
For a thicker gravy, mix 1 tsp chickpea (gram) dhal flour or cake (plain) flour with 1 Tbsp water into a fine paste. Add to the gravy with the tomato paste in step 4, stirring well.

Fish Cakes

Preparation time: 15 minutes Cooking time: 15 minutes Yields ± 15
Red Masala, Warm Masala, Three-spice Masala

Fish cakes are always a favourite, and these are crammed with the savoury delight of three masalas. They're no trouble to conjure up.

150 g (1 tin) chunky tuna in brine
1 tsp cumin seeds
¼ tsp salt
1 tsp Red Masala
¼ tsp turmeric
½ tsp Three-spice Masala
½ tsp Warm Masala
½ tsp chilli powder (optional)
¼ finely chopped onion
2 finely chopped cloves garlic
3 heaped Tbsp finely chopped fresh coriander
1 heaped Tbsp finely chopped parsley (optional)
½ Tbsp lemon juice
3 slightly stale slices white or brown bread
¼ cup water
1 large egg
oil for frying

1. Drain the tuna. Coarsely crush the cumin seeds in a mortar. Mix into the tuna with the salt, Red Masala, turmeric, Three-spice and Warm Masalas, crushed cumin seeds and chilli powder in a medium-sized bowl. Add the onion, garlic, coriander, parsley and lemon juice, and press through the tuna with a fork.

2. Break the bread into pieces and soak in the water for 2–3 minutes. Beat the egg, and squeeze the water from the bread. Add the egg and bread to the tuna, mashing all the ingredients together thoroughly. If the mixture sticks to the fingers, add an extra ½ slice bread (broken up and soaked).

3. Shape the mixture into small balls, then press between the palms into thin 4–5 cm diameter patties (less than 1 cm thick). Heat a thin layer of oil in a medium-sized, non-stick frying pan on medium-high. When hot, place as many patties into the pan as possible. Fry for 2 minutes per side, flipping twice, for a total cooking time of about 6 minutes,

until the patties are well-browned. Drain on kitchen paper.

Serve hot from the pan as finger food, or with mashed potatoes and 'Quick Coriander Chutney' (p. 24) as a more substantial snack.

Hints and variations

Tuna is a splendidly accommodating fish. There are no hard and fast rules for these cakes: if fresh herbs aren't available, add extra garlic; if you have no Red Masala, use Green; 4–5 Tbsp milk may be used in place of the egg, and so on. Just remember that the mixture should be well bound, the patties thin (less than 1 cm thick), and the frying pan unwarped.

Tea Break

Sweetmeats and hot, sweet Indian dishes –
the latter traditionally served before main courses
– make superb comfort food, ideal companions
for a stolen moment and a cup of steaming Chai.

Caution: these pages can be dangerous. In them you'll find the two masalas that preside over the seductive realm of sweet Indian cuisine. In fact, Cardamom-Nutmeg Masala (p. 120) is not a true masala at all, merely a mixture of roasted cardamom seeds and grated nutmeg. But its superlative flavour warrants its ranking with the finest spice and chilli blends. A pinch yields ambrosial fragrance and taste – the merest whiff of it causes sweet-tooth cravings!

Tea Masala (p. 118), on the other hand, is the gold dust of the true masalas, a specialised mixture for a specialised ritual, the brewing of a cup of tea. How important is tea – or Chai – in Indian culture? A hint: it's the only 'food' with its own masala! And food it deserves to be called – food for the soul. A cup of tea infused with masala (see 'Chai', p. 121) carries you expansively away, and returns you to the present invigorated and ready for anything.

The tasty treats that follow the masala recipes are both the best of the dozens of 'mithai' – Indian sweetmeats – from the easiest 'practice makes perfect!' categories, and our favourite hot, sweet Indian dishes. The latter are great anytime for a quick energy boost and try serving them in traditional style, ahead of the mains, as an authentic 'Indian dinner' touch.

Sweetmeats, meanwhile, need a watchful eye, a deft touch, and sometimes a sixth sense: as a class, they can confound even master craftsmen. The confectioneries in this book are thoroughly kitchen tested, however, and will guide you past common missteps. Always cook with liquid or softened 'Ghee' (p. 124), and use thin-bottomed pots and pans, which cool quickly when removed from heat. Sweetmeats are served during festive times, so make them colourful and merry – every morsel a mini celebration!

Tea Masala and Cardamom-Nutmeg Masala

It is somehow fitting that the most elaborate masala should be paired with the simplest recipe. The mysteries of tea – its powers to soothe and restore the psyche – remain quite unexplained, and Tea Masala has been blended for centuries in celebration of these properties. The masala complements and enhances the tea leaf, so that each cup wreathes the drinker in uplifting energy.

The predominant taste and smell of Tea Masala derive from white pepper kernels and cardamom pods, which are accompanied by a quintessential gingery, cinnamony undertone. A hint of nutmeg and rare ganthoda complete the piquant picture. A large batch of Tea Masala keeps well over time – depending on how often you share it!

Heaven, meanwhile, is a kitchen in which Cardamom-Nutmeg Masala has just been prepared. The sweet aroma of the freshly roasted cardamom, which invades every corner of the room, is utterly possessing, and one makes up excuses to linger in the heady bouquet. The spice mixture is not quite a true masala, but has a similarly all-pervasive influence on the dishes it is intended for: the hot, sweet wheat dishes and the deliciously tempting sweetmeat delicacies.

As with the other masala pairings, it's convenient to make these two together. Don't forget to reward yourself with a cup of 'Chai' (p. 121) after blending the Tea Masala, to ensure that it's to your taste.

Tea Masala

Preparation time: 40 minutes (large batch) 15 minutes (small batch)

LARGE BATCH

20 g or about 2½ Tbsp black pepper kernels
130 g or about 1 cup white pepper kernels
35 g cinnamon stick pieces, or
about ¾ cup (1–2 cm pieces)
8 small pieces ganthoda (long pepper)
(optional)
12 g/4–5 pieces dried ginger root
½ nutmeg
50 g or about ¾ cup cardamom pods
1 tsp ginger powder (see Hints and variations)
2 tsp white pepper powder (optional)
(see Hints and variations)

1. Clean and sort the black and white pepper kernels separately, removing any sticks, stones, husks or substandard kernels. (Using a white plate helps.) Toss the kernels separately in a wire strainer to sift out chaff and specks of dirt. Mix the black and white pepper on a microwave-safe dish or tray, and spread into a thin, even layer. Roast in the microwave on 200W/low/defrost for 5–6 minutes, pausing to stir three times, until the mixture radiates warmth. Set aside.

2. Break the cinnamon sticks into small bits. Roast with the ganthoda for 5–6 minutes in the microwave on 200W/low/defrost. Pound the bits in a mortar until very fine, almost powdery. Set aside.

3. Pound 4–5 pieces of dried ginger root in the mortar until fine. Sift through the wire strainer to catch the ginger fibres. Set aside.

4. Crush ½ nutmeg into small pieces in the mortar, and roast with the cardamom pods as per the cinnamon, pausing to stir twice. (See roasting caution for cardamom, p. 9.) Allow to cool until required during grinding.

5. Grind the black and white pepper kernels in three batches (stir each batch several times), until mostly fine and powdery, with a hint of coarseness when pinched. Reserve in a small bowl. Wipe the grinder clean with a dry cloth.

6. Grind the cinnamon and ganthoda in a single batch, again pausing several times to stir, until the powder has a fine sandy feel. Add to the black and white pepper, and mix in well. Wipe the grinder clean. Add the pounded ginger root to the pepper and cinnamon mixture, and stir thoroughly.

7. Grind the cardamom, pausing to stir several times, again just to the cusp of powdery fine. Pound the nutmeg to very fine in the mortar. Add both to the mixture and mix thoroughly.

Tea Masala should be a light, coarse powder with a strong peppery flavour and rich sweet smell. It keeps in a spice jar for up to 1 year.

SMALL BATCH

⅛ tsp black pepper kernels
2 tsp white pepper kernels
7–8 cinnamon stick pieces
12–14 cardamom pods
⅛ tsp grated nutmeg
½ tsp ginger powder (see Hints and variations)

1. Sort and clean all the spices as per the large-batch recipe instructions.

2. Spread the black and white pepper kernels into an even layer on a microwave-safe dish or tray. Roast in the microwave on 200W/low/defrost for 3–4 minutes. Pound in a mortar until fine. Remove and set aside.

3. Roast the cinnamon stick pieces for 2–3 minutes on 200W/low/defrost. Pound to fine in the mortar and set aside. Wipe the mortar clean.

4. Roast the cardamom pods as per the cinnamon. (See roasting caution for cardamom, p. 9.) Pound in the mortar until fine (remove any husks that do not pulverise, if desired). Add the nutmeg to the crushed cardamom.

5. Mix all the spices well, pour into the mortar, and pound for a final 30 seconds–1 minute to ensure a good consistency.

A small batch yields enough Tea Masala for 12–15 cups of tea.

Hints and variations

For a stronger Tea Masala, add extra white pepper (up to 2 tsp white pepper powder) or a pinch of ginger powder, and, for a sweeter one, more cardamom and cinnamon. Be careful when adding cinnamon, as it can overpower the masala's other tastes. For the large batch, be sure to grind the spices as called for: separate grinding (of sweet and strong spices) is very important.

Cardamom-Nutmeg Masala

Preparation time: 15 minutes (large batch) 10 minutes (small batch)

LARGE BATCH

40 g or about ½ cup cardamom pods

¾ nutmeg

1. Roast the cardamom pods for 4–5 minutes in the microwave on 200W/low/defrost, stirring the batch twice. (See roasting caution for cardamom, p. 9.) A rich, sweet aroma will waft into the kitchen. De-husk the pods: place them in three batches in a mortar, and stamp until the tiny black seeds are loose. Pour out the contents, and remove the husks. Pour the seeds into a wire-mesh strainer, and toss gently to dislodge the remaining chaff. Grind the roasted seeds in a spice mill/coffee grinder until semi-fine: sandy smooth with the occasional larger-grit pieces.

2. Grate the nutmeg into a bowl using the 'star' face of the grater, until it yields about 2½ tsp powder. Add the ground cardamom and mix thoroughly.

Keep in a spice jar in a cool, dry place. The masala's freshness and strength will keep for up to 1 year.

SMALL BATCH

1 tsp whole cardamom seeds (from about 1 Tbsp or 15–30 pods, depending on size)

⅛ tsp grated nutmeg

1. Roast the cardamom pods for 3–4 minutes in the microwave on 200W/low/defrost. (See the roasting caution for cardamom, p. 9.) De-husk as per the large-batch recipe. Pound the roasted seeds in a mortar until fine.

2. Add the nutmeg to the crushed cardamom seeds. Pound the spices together for 30 seconds–1 minute, to ensure optimum consistency.

A small batch yields enough Cardamom-Nutmeg Masala to prepare two sweetmeat or hot sweet dish recipes.

Chai

Cooking time: 5 minutes Serves 2
Tea Masala

The ritual of making Chai can be a splendidly meditative act, a perfect break to separate busy spells. Drinking it, meanwhile, is a small blessing. The sweet-smelling steam curls around you as the Tea Masala works its magic, tingling your tastebuds, delivering a boost with each sip. Chai is prepared on the stovetop, in a small pot or saucepan – it is particularly convenient to use a saucepan with a lip for pouring.

½ cup milk

1 cup water

2 Ceylon tea bags, or 3 tsp loose Ceylon tea

¼ tsp Tea Masala

2–3 lemon grass leaves, torn into small pieces (optional)

¼ tsp grated ginger (optional)

1. Heat all the ingredients in a small pot on medium-high. Bring to the boil, stirring well to ensure that the tea steeps thoroughly, and to prevent it from boiling over.

2. As soon as the liquid begins to simmer rapidly, remove the pot from the heat. Pour the contents through a fine sieve or tea strainer into tea cups or mugs. Sweeten to taste.

Serve with all manner of sweet-meats and savouries, or enjoy on its own.

Hints and variations

If you prefer herbal tea, make this recipe with rooibos instead of Ceylon. It's just as tasty!

Mango Rhas

Preparation time: 15 minutes Serves 2–4

In a chapter dedicated to sweet Indian cuisine, a recipe for mango juice? We couldn't resist including it! You can consider this refreshing drink a liquid dessert – or serve it to kick off a party on a hot summer evening. It makes a splendid, unusual guest-greeter.

2 large, ripe, stringless mangoes,
500–600 g each
juice of ½ lime (optional)
⅛ tsp salt
¼ tsp ginger powder
⅛ tsp white pepper powder

TO GARNISH
pinch chilli powder or paprika

1. Peel the mangoes, slice the flesh off the pip and place in a bowl. Discard the pip. Cut the flesh into medium-sized cubes.

2. Place the mango cubes in a liquidiser or food processor, and liquidise on medium speed to a smooth, thick liquid. Add the lime juice (optional), salt, ginger powder and white pepper powder, and blend in well. Two large mangoes yield about 750 ml very thick juice.

Chill the Rhas in the fridge, if desired. Pour into glasses, sprinkle with chilli powder or paprika, and serve. Rhas keeps for 3–4 days in the fridge, or for a longer period when frozen in an airtight container.

Hints and variations

Mangoes are at their best for Rhas upon just ripening, before they are very soft and/or syrupy sweet. Always select stringless mangoes for Rhas.

For a 'smoothie' effect, add a splash of milk when blending. An alternative method of preparing and serving Rhas turns it into a fun appetiser: liquidise the mango and lime juice only, pour it into small bowls, and serve accompanied by the spices on a spice tray, for guests to make their own combinations, and by 'Plain Soft Puri' (p. 149), for dipping and scooping.

Ghee

Cooking time: 15 minutes

In Indian culture, ghee – clarified butter – is revered as health giving food for body and soul. It is an essential ingredient in sweetmeats and hot sweet dishes, imparting to them an unmistakable, aromatic, nutty richness. Making large amounts of ghee requires great skill – but making half a kilogram is a cinch, and is as much as you're likely to need at any given time. Ghee is also now widely available in supermarkets and speciality food shops.

1. Slice 500 g butter into five equal pieces. Heat a deep saucepan on medium-high. When it is hot, add the butter piece by piece, waiting until each piece has melted before adding the next. Keep a close watch on the saucepan: the butter will froth and begin to boil. If it threatens to boil over, remove it from the heat for a few seconds.

2. After about 5 minutes of frothing/boiling, the butter will subside and reduce to a fast simmer of its own accord. When it's possible to see through the clarified liquid to the bottom of the pan, reduce the heat to medium. Stir gently to prevent scorching, and continue to simmer for about 5 minutes.

3. Inspect a spoonful of liquid: it should be golden, mostly clear, and should contain small brown suspended particles. When these particles are well browned (as opposed to white when first forming), the ghee is done. Remove from the heat. Wet your fingers with water and shake a few drops into the ghee. Allow it to cool for about 5 minutes.

4. Pour the ghee through a fine-meshed strainer into a stainless steel or earthenware container. Discard the residue and allow the ghee to cool completely.

Cover the container and keep the ghee in a cool, dark place. Ghee keeps for several months, especially in the winter, and even longer in the fridge.

Hints and variations

Check the ingredient list on the butter label before buying it: the only items should be butter (milk solids) and salt. Some butter contains water or hydrogenated oils, both of which ruin ghee.

Be sure to allow the ghee to soften well before using it in any of the recipes that follow.

Crunchy Chickpea Fudge

Preparation time: 10 minutes Cooking time: 15 minutes Serves 6–8
Cardamom-Nutmeg Masala

This is a traditional wintertime treat, but fudge lovers will consider it perfect for any season of the year!

2 cups chickpea (gram) dhal flour
11 Tbsp softened or liquid ghee
2½ Tbsp full-cream milk
¼ cup castor sugar
½ tsp Cardamom-Nutmeg Masala

TO DECORATE (OPTIONAL)
1 Tbsp almond slivers

1. Sift the flour into a wide mixing bowl. Add 1 Tbsp softened or liquid ghee and stir in. Add the milk and stir in well, until the ghee and milk are completely and evenly absorbed. Pour the flour mixture into a food processor, and blend on low speed until smooth. Alternatively, rub the flour into a bowl between your palms, forming fine, even crumbs.

2. Heat 10 Tbsp ghee in a thin-based saucepan on medium. When it is warm, add the flour mixture and stir well until evenly moist. Reduce the heat to medium-low. Stir continuously for 10–12 minutes, scraping up all the stickings to prevent scorching. As the dough braises, it becomes less dense and easier to stir. When it is very 'fluffy' and has darkened to a caramel colour, remove the saucepan from the heat.

3. Add the sugar and Cardamom-Nutmeg Masala, and stir in thoroughly. Pour the hot fudge into a small square or round baking tray (about 20 cm x 25 cm or 17 cm in diameter) lined with waxed paper. Smooth it with the back of a spoon (the top will shine as though wet). Decorate with almond slivers (optional).

Allow the fudge to cool and set outside of the fridge for about 2 hours, or until hardened. Cut into squares with a blunt, non-serrated knife. Serve at room temperature on any occasion. Store in a waxed paper-lined tin in a cool, dry place, where it will keep indefinitely.

Hints and variations
When cutting, the larger the squares, the less the crumbling. When making the fudge in summer, choose a cool time – early morning or late evening – or the heat of the day will prevent it from setting.

Easy Burfi

Preparation time: 10 minutes Cooking time: 25 minutes Serves 6–8
Cardamom-Nutmeg Masala

Burfi is a creamy delight, perhaps (and deservedly!) India's most famous sweetmeat. There are many ways to make it – we consider this recipe one of the best because of its simplicity and superb results. Be prepared to guard your burfi until serving time. Unguarded burfi rapidly disappears!

250 g powdered milk
1 cup fresh cream
1 Tbsp softened or liquid ghee
(at room temperature)
¾ cup sugar
½ cup water
5–6 strands saffron
½ tsp Cardamom-Nutmeg Masala

TO DECORATE (ALL OPTIONAL)
1 Tbsp almond slivers (plain or dyed)
silver decoration balls or foil
¼ tsp crushed cardamom seeds

1. Grease a square, medium-sized baking tray (about 20 cm x 25 cm) with butter or ghee.

2. Pour the powdered milk into a wide mixing bowl. Add the fresh cream and ghee and mix until the milk powder has formed into fine clumps. Pour the mixture into a food processor or liquidiser, and blend on low speed until finely crumbed. Alternately, pour the mixture into a large wire-mesh strainer one handful at a time, and rub through the mesh. (The end result of either process resembles couscous in shape and colour.) Reserve.

3. Pour the sugar into a medium-sized, thin-based saucepan and add the water. Heat the saucepan and stir to help the sugar dissolve. When the water reaches a rapid simmer, reduce the heat. Add the saffron and simmer for 5–6 minutes, until the sugar water reduces to a slightly sticky, thin, golden syrup. (To test the stickiness, remove a small sample with a teaspoon, allow it to cool, and then touch. Never touch caramelising sugar in a hot pot or pan, or immediately after it has been removed.)

4. Reduce the heat to low. Add the milk powder crumbs and stir thoroughly into the syrup. Add the Cardamom-Nutmeg Masala and stir. Cook for 10–12 minutes, stirring continuously to prevent scorching. When the liquid mixture begins to bubble, and swift strokes with a spoon whip the mixture stiffly back, drawing it without streaks across the base of the pan, remove it from the heat. Pour it into the baking tray, spread it out evenly and smooth the top with a spatula.

5. While the burfi is still warm, garnish it as desired with dyed almonds, crushed cardamom seeds, and so on. Allow it to cool and set, preferably overnight. Do not cool the burfi in the fridge.

Cut into squares and serve at room temperature. Keep in a waxed paper-lined tin – not an airtight container. Burfi made with fresh cream keeps for a few days outside of the fridge, and for up to 2 weeks inside.

Hints and variations

If your burfi is too soft or too dry, make adjustments the next time: if the burfi is dry, add a few Tbsp full-cream milk during step 4; if it's wet and shapeless, increase the cooking time. For a rich, pale golden colour, add a few millilitres saffron syrup with the sugar in step 3.

Fine Sweet Sev

Preparation time: 5 minutes Cooking time: 15–20 minutes Serves 4
Cardamom-Nutmeg Masala

This hot, sweet dish gives off a wonderful, buttery, cinnamony aroma during cooking. Serve it Indian style before a main course, with vanilla ice cream as a dessert, or as a superb tea-time snack.

200 g super-fine vermicelli
3 Tbsp ghee or butter
7–10 cinnamon stick pieces
1½ cup freshly boiled water
¼ cup sugar
½ tsp Cardamom-Nutmeg Masala
1 Tbsp sultanas (optional)
1 Tbsp almond slivers (optional)

1. Crush the vermicelli with your hands in a large mixing bowl until the noodles are broken into small, 1 cm bits.

2. Heat the butter or ghee in a small saucepan on medium-low. Add the cinnamon sticks as it melts.

3. Add the vermicelli to the melted butter, and stir until well coated. As it warms, the pasta will begin to 'crackle'. Stir continuously for 5–7 minutes, until the pasta has darkened to a golden brown with a pink glow, and gives off a pleasant roasted aroma.

4. Raise the heat to medium. Carefully add 1 cup of freshly boiled water (it will hiss and splutter when added) and stir through the pasta. Add another ½ cup water, so that it just covers the pasta. Cover and simmer for 5 minutes, stirring occasionally to prevent sticking.

5. When the pasta is soft, stir in the sugar, Cardamom-Nutmeg Masala, sultanas and almond slivers. Cover the saucepan and simmer for a final 3–5 minutes, until the water has completely evaporated and the vermicelli is cooked through.

Enjoy anytime!

Doodhpak

Preparation time: 5 minutes Cooking time: 45 minutes Serves 4–6
Cardamom-Nutmeg Masala

This luscious hot liquid is like a pourable sweetmeat. It's simple to make and fun to serve, especially as a winter warmer instead of coffee. During Indian meals, it is traditionally served ahead of a main dish, but it follows nicely, too!

1 litre full-cream milk
⅛ cup basmati rice
20 g super-fine vermicelli (about ¼ cup crushed)
½ tsp ghee
¼ cup sugar
2–3 strands saffron
½ tsp Cardamom-Nutmeg Masala
1 Tbsp crushed almond slivers
2–3 coarsely chopped pistachios

1. Allow the milk to stand outside of the fridge for 15–20 minutes before starting, so that it reaches room temperature. Rinse and soak the basmati rice at the same time. Drain the rice well before starting the dish.

2. Crush the vermicelli in a large bowl with your hands, until evenly broken up into 2–3 cm long noodles.

3. Heat the ghee in a small saucepan on medium. When hot, add the vermicelli and stir in well. Stir continuously for 3 minutes, until the pasta is well braised and has acquired a rosy or pinkish colour. Remove the saucepan from the heat.

4. Pour the milk into a deep, medium-sized pot, place it on the hot stove-plate, and raise the heat to medium-high. Stir frequently until the milk is near boiling point. When it begins to steam and it bubbles at the sides of the pot, stir in the braised vermicelli. Stir continuously until the milk returns to a simmer.

5. Reduce the heat to low. Add the rice and stir in. Simmer the milk on medium-low for 30 minutes, stirring frequently (keep the spoon in the pot), until it has reduced in volume by approximately two-thirds. Any thickened milk that forms on the top may be stirred back into the pot.

6. Remove the pot from the heat. Add the sugar, saffron, Cardamom-Nutmeg Masala, almond slivers and pistachios, and stir in well.

Serve warm in small bowls with 'Plain Soft Puri' (p. 149) for dipping. Once cooled, keep Doodhpak in the fridge for up to 2 days. Reheat only once. To reheat, bring to a simmer on the stove, stirring in any thickened milk that forms on top. Guard against boiling over. Serve as soon as the simmering starts.

Lapshi

Cooking time: 30 minutes Serves 4
Cardamom-Nutmeg Masala

This sweet, steaming crushed wheat dish is traditionally served ahead of a main course, but we've found that it also makes a delicious hot breakfast, especially in wintertime. It's filling and energy giving, with the lovely aroma of fennel.

1 Tbsp ghee
3–4 cinnamon stick pieces
½ cup crushed wheat
2 cups freshly boiled water
¼ tsp fennel seeds
3 Tbsp sugar
¼ tsp Cardamom-Nutmeg Masala
1 Tbsp almond slivers (optional)

1. Heat the ghee in a medium-sized saucepan on medium. Add the cinnamon sticks as the ghee melts. When the liquid begins to 'simmer', add the crushed wheat, and stir continuously for 4–5 minutes, until it yields a rich, wheaty aroma.

2. Reduce the heat. Carefully add the freshly boiled water (it will hiss and splutter when added) and stir. Cover and simmer for about 20 minutes, until the wheat is soft and most of the water has evaporated. Stir every 5 minutes, adding water by the quarter cupful if necessary to prevent scorching. A sweet aroma will fill the kitchen, and the wheat will take on a pinkish hue.

3. Stir in the fennel seeds, sugar, Cardamom-Nutmeg Masala and almond slivers (optional). Cover and steam for an additional 3–4 minutes, until the water is fully evaporated and only the moist wheat mixture remains.

Enjoy anytime!

Hints and variations
Lapshi reheats particularly well in the microwave. It can be made in the amount called for here, and enjoyed on several successive chilly mornings!

Sheero

Preparation time: 5 minutes Cooking time: 20 minutes Serves 2–4
Cardamom-Nutmeg Masala

This is a simple recipe that yields a smooth and creamy hot treat. It is traditionally served ahead of a main course, but we like it best during Chai-time!

½ cup hot water
2 Tbsp ghee or butter
4–5 cinnamon stick pieces
½ cup semolina
½ cup full-cream milk
¼ cup sugar
½ tsp Cardamom-Nutmeg Masala
½ Tbsp chopped almond slivers (optional)
1 heaped Tbsp sultanas (optional)

1. Boil enough water in a kettle to yield ½ cup, and allow to cool during step 2.

2. Heat the ghee or butter in a medium-sized pot on medium. Add the cinnamon sticks. When sizzling, reduce the heat, add the semolina, and stir continuously for 7–9 minutes, until golden brown. A lovely baked, wheaty aroma will fill the kitchen.

3. Remove the pot from the heat, leaving the stoveplate on low. Mix the milk and hot water in a cup, and pour into the pot carefully (the liquid will hiss and splutter as it is added). Stir well. Add the sugar and Cardamom-Nutmeg Masala, and stir again. Add the almond slivers and sultanas, and stir.

4. Return the pot to the stove. Cover and steam for 4–5 minutes, until the liquid has been completely absorbed and the semolina is firm. Remove from the heat.

Break up and fluff with a spoon. Serve hot.

Hints and variations
It's best to buy the highest-grade brand-name semolina available, because the cheaper semolinas tend to contain tiny bits of millstone.

Naankhataai

Preparation time: 15 minutes Cooking time: 15–20 minutes Serves 4–6 Yields 30
Cardamom-Nutmeg Masala

These lovely melt-in-the-mouth baked biscuits (pronounced 'NON-kha-tie') are very light and firm, and crumble deliciously when popped into the mouth. They make a superb vehicle for the sweet flavour of cardamom.

½ cup + 2 Tbsp
softened ghee (room temperature)
⅜ **cup sugar**
½ **tsp Cardamom-Nutmeg Masala**
1 **heaped Tbsp semolina**
2 **cups cake (plain) flour**
¼ **tsp baking powder**
⅛ **tsp bicarbonate of soda**

TO DECORATE (OPTIONAL)
almond slivers
silver decoration balls

1. Pre-heat the oven to a moderate 180 °C/350 °F/Gas mark 4.

2. Pour the ghee into a wide mixing bowl. Add the sugar and mix with a whisk until thoroughly creamed. Add the Cardamom-Nutmeg Masala and semolina, stirring well.

3. Sift the flour into a separate bowl, then mix in the baking powder and bicarbonate of soda. Add a third of this dry mixture to the sugar and ghee mixture, and stir until completely absorbed. Repeat with the second third of the dry mixture. Add the final third, and knead it with your hands into a creamy dough.

4. Separate the dough into about 30 equal pieces, rolling them between your palms into slightly flat balls, about 3 cm in diameter and 2 cm thick. Place the balls close together in rows on an ungreased, rectangular baking tray. Decorate minimally, if desired, pressing almond slivers or silver balls lightly into each ball of dough.

5. Place the tray in the oven and bake for 15–20 minutes, until the biscuits are golden and firm, with small cracks on top. Remove before they begin to brown on top (or they'll be overdone).

Remove the tray and allow to cool. Lift the Naankhataai with a spatula. Serve warm or at room temperature. Keep in a waxed paper-lined tin for up to 2 weeks.

Shrikhand

Preparation time: 30 minutes Draining time: 12–14 hours Reserving time: 1 hour
Cooking time: 20 minutes Serves 6–8
Cardamom-Nutmeg Masala

Some call this dish 'Indian ice cream'. It's the pinnacle of creamy sweetmeat richness. Although the instructions for making it are quite straightforward, the labour involved is fairly substantial, and properly made Shrikhand requires good planning ahead. See the note following the recipe for a shortcut that utterly deflates these warnings!

1 litre buttermilk
sugar for sprinkling
375 g (1½ tubs) full-cream plain
smooth cottage cheese
¾ cup sugar
10 strands saffron
1 tsp Cardamom-Nutmeg Masala

TO GARNISH (ALL OPTIONAL)
4–5 chopped pistachios
2 Tbsp chopped almond slivers
edible foil

1. Line a wide mixing bowl with doubled-over butter muslin, so that the cloth drapes over the lip of the bowl. Shake the buttermilk carton well, and pour the buttermilk into the lined bowl. Gather the ends of the cloth and tie loosely. Suspend the bundle over the bowl for 12–14 hours. The buttermilk will be reduced to a curd less than half its original size and weight. Discard the water that collects in the bowl.

2. Remove all the curd from the cloth with a spatula and place in a bowl. Wrap a second, smaller bowl or casserole dish with the same cloth, pulling it semi-tightly over the mouth. Place the curd 4 Tbsp at a time on to the centre of the cloth. Sprinkle each batch of curd with 1 tsp sugar. Press and scrape the curd through the cloth with the back of a spoon. When finished, scrape the cloth clean on both sides, bunch it and squeeze out any remaining curd.

3. Mix the cottage cheese and sugar into the curd, 2 Tbsp cottage cheese and 1 Tbsp sugar at a time. (Mix in each added portion well before adding the next portion.) When this is done, add the saffron strands and Cardamom-Nutmeg Masala and stir in thoroughly. Scoop the entire mixture into a serving dish.

Sprinkle with pistachios and almonds and reserve in the fridge. Let the mixture stand for a minimum of one hour to allow it to absorb the saffron and masala flavours. Decorate with edible foil and serve chilled with 'Plain Soft Puri' (p. 149). Shrikhand keeps in the fridge for up to 1 week.

Hints and variations

If you simply must have your Indian ice cream right now, here's a tip from us that borders on Indian culinary heresy: replace the buttermilk with 125 ml fresh cream and leave out step 1 entirely. Reduce the sugar amount to 6 heaped Tbsp. Place all the ingredients in a bowl and mix well with an electric mixer until stiff. Garnish as you please. The dish won't be 'pure' Shrikhand, but will still be pure bliss to eat!

Goolaab Jamboo

Preparation time: 20 minutes Reserving time: 20 minutes Cooking time: 30 minutes
Serves 4–6 Yields 30
Cardamom-Nutmeg Masala

This outrageously rich, sweet and sticky Indian delight is an ingenious creation. It requires a sharp eye – you may want to become comfortable with 'Easy Burfi' (p. 126) first, and then move on to Goolaab Jamboo. But it's not that difficult – go on, just dive right in!

200 g (1 tin) full-cream condensed milk (sweetened)
2 Tbsp liquid ghee at room temperature
1 heaped tsp Cardamom-Nutmeg Masala
1½ cups cake (plain) flour
¼ cup semolina
1¼ tsp baking powder
4 Tbsp full-cream milk
1½ cups water
1½ cups sugar
2–3 drops rose essence (optional)
butter for greasing
flour for dusting
oil for light frying

1. Prepare the dough: pour the condensed milk into a large mixing bowl, add the ghee and Cardamom-Nutmeg Masala, and mix well. Sift the cake flour into a separate bowl, then add the semolina and baking powder, and mix well. Add the dry ingredients to the wet ingredients, add the milk, and mix thoroughly. Cover the bowl with a cloth and reserve the dough for 20 minutes.

2. Prepare the syrup: pour the water into a medium-sized saucepan, add the sugar and rose essence, and bring to a rapid simmer on high, stirring well to dissolve the sugar. Reduce the heat, and simmer for 8–10 minutes, until the water has reduced to about half the volume, resulting in a thin syrup. Switch off the heat, leaving the syrup on the stove top to ensure that it stays warm.

3. Grease a rectangular baking tray and dust it lightly with flour. Pour about 1 tsp oil into a finger bowl. Knead the dough, ensuring that any areas that have dried are incorporated into the moist core. Twist off very small balls of dough, about 1.5 cm in diameter. Roll the balls between your palms into 'cylinders' that are plump in the middle and taper at the ends, about 5 cm long. Dip your fingers in the finger bowl to prevent them from sticking to the dough. Place the cylinders on a greased tray and cover with waxed paper.

4. Heat the oil to a depth of about 1 cm in a medium-sized saucepan on medium-low. Test the oil with a bit of dough to determine readiness: if it bubbles and skates slowly around the pan, the oil is ready. If necessary, re-shape the dough cylinders between your palms. Place the cylinders in the oil, 4–5 at a time, allow to brown (bubbling and expanding) for 30 seconds. Turn with a fork, and fry for another 30 seconds. Turn twice

more, until cracks form in the cylinders' thick middles, and they are well-browned on all sides. Place the fried cylinders into the syrup pot immediately, and allow to soak for 30 seconds. Remove and drain on kitchen paper. Fry and dip the remaining batches, adding more oil if necessary to finish.

Serve at room temperature. Keep the Goolab Jamboo in a waxed paper-lined tin (outside of the fridge) for up to 2 weeks.

Hints and variations

The highest-grade semolina is best for this recipe, because cheaper semolinas tend to contain specks of millstone. If your Goolaab Jamboo, when cut in half, has a very white centre, then the dough hasn't cracked open enough during frying to allow the syrup to soak completely through. Increase the frying time slightly.

Rice and Breads

Plain, steaming rice makes the perfect
accompaniment to most curries. Roti and other
flatbreads are hearty hallmarks of Indian
cuisine. This chapter has just one simple rule –
make enough!

rice breads roti

If you aren't already old friends, it's time to become acquainted with basmati rice, which is what many Indian chefs refer to when they simply say 'rice'. Basmati is a long, thin, quick-cooking grain, among the most nutritious of the 'white' rices. It's wonderful served plain, but also carries colour and flavour superbly – hence the delicious variations, 'Aromatic Rice' (p. 144) and 'Savoury Rice' (p. 146) presented here. (And don't forget that there is another recipe in this book which virtually qualifies as a rice recipe, too: the gourmet 'Prawn Biryani', p. 106).

From rice we move to the staff of life, bread! We've brought you recipes from the same culinary tradition which produced the masala system itself: the Gujerati tradition. The 'Classic Roti' (p. 147) undoubtedly deserves first rank among the several pleasing varieties here – many consider it to be the embodiment of goodness. But it has close rivals in the goodness stakes! Each of the bread recipes, we'll bet, is sure to start a friendly competition when the results are served.

Plain Rice

Preparation time: 30 minutes Cooking time: 20 minutes Serves 4

Indian basmati rice is highly nutritious, quick cooking and splendidly aromatic. It absorbs flavours and aromas very well, and may be served with almost any dish, not just those in this book. If you're comfortable with your own method of cooking rice, stick to it. This method is very good if you haven't got one.

2 cups basmati rice
water for soaking
3 cups water
2 tsp salt
4–5 cinnamon stick pieces

1. Place the dry rice in a bowl, cover with water, and stir to dislodge starchy dust. Drain. (You may simply pour the water off the rice, rather than drain it completely in a colander.) Repeat this once. Cover the rice with fresh water, and soak for 30 minutes.

2. Drain the rice in a colander. Bring 3 cups of water to the boil in a medium-sized pot. Add the soaked rice to the boiling water with the salt and cinnamon sticks. Bring the water back to the boil, reduce the heat to low and partially cover the pot. Cook for 7–10 minutes (watch the pot closely for the first few minutes, in case the rice begins to boil over) until the water has completely evaporated and the rice is thoroughly tender.

Serve hot with most Indian dishes.

Hints and variations

For a nice touch, add a blob of ghee to each bowl served. For lemon-coloured rice, add a pinch of turmeric with the salt in step 2. For extra-fragrant rice, to be served especially with meat and poultry, add a few strands of saffron with the salt.

If perfect rice always seems to elude you, prepare it as follows: soak and drain as indicated in step 1, pour into a large pot, cover with plenty of water (5–7 cups), add salt and cinnamon sticks, and bring to the boil on high. When boiling, reduce the heat to medium-low, partially cover, and simmer until the grains are thoroughly cooked (they will still be covered with water). Drain the cooked rice thoroughly in a colander, and return to the pot to keep warm.

Aromatic Rice

Preparation time: 20 minutes, including soaking Cooking time : 20 minutes Serves 2–4

This is a rice dish that is a meal on its own! It also makes a great accompaniment to most curries and dhals.

1 cup basmati rice
3–4 strands saffron
1 Tbsp ghee or butter
½ cup fresh or frozen peas
1¼ cup freshly boiled water
¾ tsp salt

PAN SPICES
2 cardamom pods
3–4 cinnamon stick pieces
1 whole clove

1. Rinse, soak and drain the rice as per 'Plain Rice' (p. 143). Soak the saffron in ½ Tbsp hot water. Gently tamp the cardamom pods with a pestle until they crack. (Do not split them open completely.)

2. Heat the butter or ghee in a deep pot on medium-high. Add the cardamom pods, cinnamon sticks and clove, and stir. When sizzling, reduce the heat to medium. Add the peas, stir, and braise, uncovered, for 2–3 minutes.

3. Add the soaked rice and stir thoroughly but gently, careful not to mash the peas. Stir and braise for 3–4 minutes.

4. Reduce the heat to low. Add the freshly boiled water, salt and saffron strands. Cover and steam for 15–20 minutes, until the rice is thoroughly cooked and the water has completely evaporated. Stir gently every 5 minutes to prevent scorching. Add water by the quarter cupful if extra time is required to cook the rice.

Remove the pot from the heat. Serve the rice with most dishes, fluffing it with a fork before serving.

Hints and variations
The more ghee you use, the more aromatic the result.

Savoury Rice

Have leftover rice? This recipe turns the cold white lumps in yesterday's pot into a hot savoury feast in almost no time. A highly recommended rice dish.

3 cups cooked basmati rice
(about ¾ cup uncooked)
1 Tbsp ghee or butter
½ finely chopped onion
½ tsp Green Masala
¼ tsp turmeric
1 Tbsp water
½ tsp salt

PAN SPICES
3–4 cinnamon stick pieces
2 cardamom pods
½ tsp cumin seeds
3–4 torn or lightly crushed curry leaves
(fresh or dried)

TO GARNISH
2 Tbsp finely chopped fresh coriander

1. Cook rice if necessary (see 'Plain Rice', p. 143). Gently tamp the cardamom pods with a pestle until they crack. (Do not allow the pods to split open completely.)

2. Heat the ghee or butter in a medium-sized frying pan on medium. Add the cinnamon sticks, cardamom pods, crushed cumin seeds and curry leaves. Stir well. When sizzling, add the onion, cover and braise for 3–5 minutes until golden brown and thoroughly cooked. Stir occasionally.

3. Reduce the heat. Add the Green Masala and turmeric and stir. Add the rice, sprinkle with the water, and turn carefully through the onion and spices. Cover and steam for 5 minutes, stirring twice. The rice will begin to crackle. Sprinkle with salt, and remove from the heat.

Garnish with fresh coriander. Serve hot as a main dish with 'Green Masala Buttermilk' (p. 27), or as a side dish to accompany gravy curries.

Hints and variations
Feel free to mash the rice up a bit during cooking. This adds to its tasty goodness!

Classic Roti

Preparation time: 20 minutes Cooking time: 10 minutes Serves 4 Yields 8–9

Fresh hot rotis are marvellously wholesome, the perfect accompaniment to curry morsels and spoonfuls of thick dhal. If there's one bread to master making, it's roti.

2 cups cake (plain) flour
½ tsp salt
2 Tbsp oil
6 Tbsp freshly boiled water
flour for dusting

1. Sift the flour into a wide bowl. Add the salt and stir. Add the oil and press it through the flour with the back of a spoon, until small clumps form. Add the water one Tbsp at a time, mixing each Tbsp into the flour thoroughly, first with a spoon, and then, as the dough forms, by kneading it with your hands. The desired result is a soft, moist ball.

2. Divide the ball into eight equal pieces. Roll each piece between your palms into smaller balls. Dust a rolling board with flour, press the balls flat between your palms, and roll each one into a 15 cm disc. (Re-dust the board between discs.) Lay the discs out flat, and cover with a dry cloth.

3. Select the first disc and roll it out further until very thin (18–20 cm in diameter). Repeat with the others in the order they were first rolled.

4. Heat a griddle on high. When very hot, place a disc on it, allow it to cook for about 5 seconds, then flip it with your hands or a fork. The roti will immediately begin to bubble and puff up. Using a clean, dry cloth, gently press the large air bubbles down to spread hot air inside the roti. Leave the second side on the griddle for about 20 seconds, then flip again. Continue to pat with the cloth for about 10 seconds, flip once more, and pat for a final 10 seconds. The roti is done when brown freckles appear evenly on both sides. If any roti edges are thick, press them firmly into the hot griddle with the cloth, so that they cook.

Stack the rotis pancake style, and cover with a dry cloth to keep warm. Rotis are delicious fresh off the griddle, especially with a blob of ghee or butter.

Plain Soft Puri

Preparation time: 20 minutes Cooking time: 15 minutes Serves 4–6 Yields 25

Puri is among the most versatile of the Indian flatbreads. It's close to bite sized, and excellent for dipping into gravies or spooning up a tasty vegetable or bit of meat. This is the first of three puri recipes, and represents the variation which is most often made in Indian households, because it is well-suited for both sweet and savoury dishes.

1 cup cake (plain) flour
1½ Tbsp oil or liquid ghee
(at room temperature)
½ tsp salt
¼ cup water
flour for rolling
oil for frying

1. Sift the flour into a wide mixing bowl. Add the oil or ghee and press through the flour with your fingers or the back of a spoon, until the flour is crumbly. Stir in the salt. Add the water and work it through the flour with your hands, until a dry dough results which sticks to your fingers, but is well-bound internally and does not flake. Add extra water by the ½ Tbsp if necessary to moisten the dough.

2. Twist off small pieces of dough and roll them into 1.5 cm balls (about 25). Flatten the balls slightly with your palms. Dust a rolling board lightly with flour. Roll the balls out into thin 6 cm diameter discs. Keep them covered with a damp cloth while completing the rolling.

3. Heat a small, heavy-based frying pan or pot on high. Pour in enough oil to cover the base to a depth of 0.5–1 cm. Test the oil with a small cutting of puri dough: if it bubbles and rises, the oil is ready.

4. Reduce the heat to medium-high. Place 4–5 puri discs into the hot oil, and press down lightly with the back of a fork. Fry the first side for 1 minute, flip and fry the second side for 30 seconds. Puris will puff up quickly and turn golden brown. Remove and drain on kitchen paper. Add more oil to the pan to complete the batch if necessary.

Serve hot or cooled with a variety of dishes, especially 'dry' curries.

Hints and variations
In a hurry? Divide the large dough ball into 6 equal pieces, shape into smaller balls, and roll each out until very thin. Use a pastry cutter to cut out diamond shapes; fry these instead of the discs.

Sweet Puri

Preparation time: 20 minutes Cooking time: 15 minutes Yields 20–22

This is the second of our three puri recipes, a speciality puri most often served like a sweet biscuit with tea. Note that following the exact ghee-to-oil proportion is essential here.

½ tsp moistened sesame seeds (optional)
1 cup cake (plain) flour
1 tsp ghee
2 tsp oil
½ tsp sugar
pinch salt
8 Tbsp water
flour for rolling
oil for frying

1. Place the sesame seeds in a tea strainer, moisten under a running tap, and allow to drain. Sift the flour into a wide bowl. Add the ghee, oil, sugar, salt and sesame seeds, and press through the flour with the back of a spoon until it becomes crumbly. Add the first 4 Tbsp water and mix thoroughly into the flour. Add the remaining 4 Tbsp, kneading the flour into a firm dough.

2. Pinch off small pieces of dough and shape into oval balls, about 2.5 cm long, 1.5 cm thick (20–22 in total). Keep the balls covered in a bowl. Dust a rolling board with flour. Flatten the dough balls between your palms and roll them out into 7 cm diameter discs. Lay out the discs for frying, covered with a dry cloth.

3. Pour the oil to a depth of between 0.5 and 1 cm into a medium-sized pot, and heat on medium. When hot, reduce the heat to medium-low. Place the discs in the oil 4–5 at a time. They will immediately sizzle and puff up. Quickly press them down into the oil with the back of a fork several times. Flip and repeat. The total frying time for each side should be about 15 seconds. If the discs fail to puff up, add more oil to the pot, and allow it to reach frying temperature. Drain the puri in a bowl lined with kitchen paper and keep covered while frying the others. The discs will emerge crispy, but will soften within minutes. Add more oil if necessary to complete the frying.

Puri is best served as soon as possible after frying. It keeps for several days in a waxed paper-lined tin.

Hints and variations
Extra dough can be rolled out thinly, cut into diamond shapes with a pastry cutter, and fried with the discs (see photograph right).

Crispy Puri

Preparation time: 40 minutes Cooking time: 15 minutes Serves 6–8 Yields 35–40
Green Masala

This is a classic savoury usually served with tea, or as a pre-meal snack. It requires a bit more patience than the other two puri recipes, but is well worth the effort.

1 tsp moistened sesame seeds
(optional but recommended)
¾ tsp cumin seeds
1 cup cake (plain) flour
2 tsp semolina
2 tsp cornflour
¾ tsp salt
½ tsp Green Masala
pinch of turmeric
5 tsp ghee or oil
3 Tbsp water
oil for frying

1. Rinse the sesame seeds in a fine sieve, drain and reserve for use while still moist. Coarsely crush the cumin seeds in a mortar.

2. Sift the cake flour into a wide mixing bowl. Add the semolina, cornflour and sesame seeds, mixing well. Add the salt, crushed cumin seeds, Green Masala and turmeric. Stir thoroughly.

3. Add the ghee or oil and press through with the back of a spoon, until the dough clumps together when squeezed in a fist. Add 3 Tbsp water, a Tbsp at a time, working it through for a very stiff dough. Knead well. The dough should not stick when touched. Pinch off small pieces and roll them between the palms into 2–3 cm diameter balls (35–40 in total). Flatten the balls slightly and reserve for rolling.

4. Roll the balls out into 7 cm diameter discs. (Note: do not dust the rolling board with flour.) Cut three short, parallel slits into each disc, set aside, leaving them uncovered.

5. Pour the oil to a depth of 1 cm in a small pot, and heat on medium-high. Place the discs in the oil 4 or 5 at a time. Turn with a fork every 15 seconds, until they darken slightly (total frying time 45 seconds–1 minute). Remove from the pot and drain on kitchen paper. If the discs puff up, they are too thick. (Note that all the discs will bubble to some degree, but a noticeable puffing out is undesirable.) Add oil if necessary to complete the frying.

Serve hot or at room temperature. Crispy Puri keeps for up to 2 weeks in a waxed paper-lined tin.

Hints and variations

This puri can be made without Green Masala; simply add an extra ½ tsp salt. Extra dough can be rolled out thinly and cut into diamond shapes with a pastry cutter, then fried with the discs.

Savoury Yoghurt Bites

Preparation time: 15 minutes Rising time 6–12 hours Cooking time: 20 minutes Serves 6–8 Yields 40
Green Masala, Three-spice Masala

These chewy, gumdrop-sized fried breads are the ultimate savoury snack. They tend to march out of the kitchen as quickly as you can make them! The Green and Three-spice Masalas combine with the sourness of the yoghurt to pack more flavour into each tiny bite than seems possible.

½ cup maize meal
1 cup cake (plain) flour
1 Tbsp chickpea (gram) dhal flour
⅛ tsp baking powder
1¼ tsp salt
⅛ tsp turmeric
1 tsp Three-spice Masala
1 Tbsp oil
1 Tbsp lemon juice
7 Tbsp plain yoghurt
½ tsp sesame seeds (optional)
½ tsp Green Masala
3 Tbsp water
1 heaped Tbsp finely chopped fresh coriander
⅛ tsp bicarbonate of soda
oil for frying

1. Mix the maize meal, cake flour, chickpea flour and baking powder in a deep bowl. Add the salt, turmeric and Three-spice Masala and stir. Add the oil and lemon juice and mix in well. Add the yoghurt, sesame seeds, Green Masala and water, and mix thoroughly into a dry dough. Once the water is absorbed, knead well. Add the fresh coriander, work it through the dough, and knead for a final 2–3 minutes. Cover the bowl and reserve in a warm place for a minimum of 6 hours, or overnight.

2. Knead the risen dough, adding the bicarbonate of soda. Pinch off small pieces of dough, and roll them between your palms into 2–3 cm diameter balls (about 40). Keep them covered under waxed paper before frying.

3. Heat the oil to a depth of 1 cm in a small pot on medium-high. Drop the balls into the oil, fry for 1 minute, flip with a fork, and fry until they are an even golden brown. Fry as many as 15 at a time. Remove and drain in a kitchen paper-lined bowl.

Serve warm or at room temperature. These bites are great for picnics. They keep for up to 1 week in a waxed paper-lined tin.

Foulka

Compared with our other bread recipes, this one constitutes a bit of a challenge. For one thing, yeast is involved, as is quite a lot of rolling. But, ah – the crispy-chewy, savoury result!

4 tsp warm water
2 tsp instant dry yeast
⅛ tsp sugar
4 cups cake (plain) flour
1½ tsp salt
5 Tbsp oil
1 heaped tsp whole cumin seeds
2½ tsp sugar
about 1 cup warm water
flour for dusting
oil for frying

1. Prepare the yeast: pour 4 tsp warm water into a small bowl, add 2 tsp instant dry yeast and ⅛ tsp sugar. Reserve for a few minutes until the yeast begins foaming.

2. Sift the cake flour into a large, deep mixing bowl. Add the salt and oil and work through the flour with the back of a spoon, until the flour becomes crumbly. Add the cumin seeds, 2½ tsp sugar and the foaming yeast, and stir in well. Add the warm water by the quarter cupful, kneading through the flour until a very soft and slightly sticky dough results. (The entire cup of water may not be used.) Knead the dough for several minutes to work the yeast through, and shape into a large ball. Press the ball flat into a pancake-like disc. Cover and reserve in a warm place for a minimum of 6 hours, preferably overnight. The dough will rise and more than double in volume.

3. Dust a rolling board with flour. Remove a quarter of the dough from the bowl, shape it into a ball, and press it flat on a rolling board. Roll out to a 26–28 cm diameter disc, about 0.25 cm thick. Using a glass (5–7 cm in diameter), press discs out of the dough. Gather the remaining dough and reserve. Sprinkle flour over a baking tray, place the discs on the tray, and cover with a dry cloth to prevent from drying out. Repeat with the remaining three-quarters of dough, then repeat with the off-cuts.

4. Pour oil to a depth of 1 cm into a medium-sized pot and heat on medium. When hot, place 5–6 discs in at a time. They will immediately begin to puff up. Turn with a fork or slotted spoon after 1 minute – the underside will be golden brown. Fry the second side for 1 minute, then remove and drain in a bowl lined with kitchen paper. Cover to keep warm. Repeat with the remaining discs. Add more oil to complete the frying only when the original oil has drained away almost completely.

Serve warm with 'Mince Kebabs' (p. 81) and 'Thick Tomato Chutney' (p. 26). Foulka keeps for 4–5 days in an airtight container. (Do not store in the fridge.)

Hints and variations

Reheat foulka in the microwave on low power – or toast them lightly.

Index

Page numbers in **bold** type indicate photographs.